CareerTrack
Publications

Taking Control Of Your Time And Your Life

Dick Lohr

CareerTrack Publications

CareerTrack, Inc., Publisher
3080 Center Green Drive
Boulder, Colorado 80301

Manufactured in the United States of America
10 9 8 7 6 5 4 3 2 1

ISBN 1-55977-398-7

ACKNOWLEDGEMENTS

I want to acknowledge those members of the CareerTrack corporate staff who directly and indirectly contributed to the form and presentation of this book and who tactfully and gently guided me away from those literary traps that have ensnared many an author. I want also to acknowledge those members of the CareerTrack trainer corps whose time management advice and suggestions over the years have helped me crystallize my thinking about the key time management issues that form the substance of this book. Their wisdom will help countless individuals to lead far better and more rewarding lives. Although too numerous to mention individually here, all of these wonderful people helped to make this book possible and I am most grateful to each of them.

There are several individuals that I absolutely must mention by name because of the magnitude of their contribution to the publication of this book. First, Jeff Hildebrandt for his management of this project and his writing and editing. Gillian Segal and John Lawson for their rewriting and editing work. Liz Wenzel and Brian Larkowski for their layout and design. Patricia LeChevalier, Kelly Davis and Loralee Greene for their proofreading and editorial expertise. And finally, Christa Isenhart and Bonnie Bird for coordinating the production and printing of this book.

To my wife, Jackie, and our four sons,
Rick, Tom, Bryan and Greg, who gave their
unwavering love, support and understanding as I built
my speaking career and labored over this book.
None of it would have been possible without them.

CONTENTS

Introduction 1

Maintaining Balance 4

Goal Setting 18

Organizing and Prioritizing 28

The Daily Plan 42

Organizing Your Office and Desk 54

Maintaining Control 63

Delegation 76

Controlling Meetings 85

Procrastination 94

Conclusion 102

Bibliography 104

INTRODUCTION

Do you ever wish you could find more time in a day? Most people do. Do you accomplish everything you want and need to do every day? Most people don't.

Today more than ever, time management skills are at the core of any success — personal or professional. With shrinking organizations, increasing workloads, dwindling resources, mandates for high quality, demanding customers, heightened competition and pleas for volunteerism, you will inevitably find yourself overwhelmed ... unless you learn how to make better use of your time.

I've worked in the training industry for nearly 15 years and have trained more than 100,000 people in the art and science of time management. I've never met anyone who was born with the ability to manage time effectively. Time management is a learned skill, an acquired talent. Fortunately, it's not difficult to master.

This book was written to provide you with the mind-set, skills and techniques to maximize the use of your precious time. Besides equipping you with the knowledge you'll need to use your time wisely, this book will also show you a process for maintaining balance and sanity in your life — especially during times when you find yourself in the midst of utter chaos.

10 time-eaters

Most time management problems can be traced to these personal and professional time-eaters:

1. Lack of objectives, priorities and planning
2. Attempting too much
3. Lack of self-discipline
4. Crisis management and shifting priorities
5. Inability to say no
6. Interruptions (telephone, drop-in visitors, etc.)
7. Personal disorganization
8. Meetings
9. Ineffective delegation
10. Procrastination

All of these time leeches can consume your workday, your evenings, even your weekends, leaving you exhausted and frustrated when you can't accomplish what you want and need to do. You've probably had large chunks of your time sucked away by the unproductive weekly staff meeting, the sudden crisis that demands immediate attention, the unwanted telephone interruption and the office visitor who refuses to leave. The good news is that you can often eliminate these problems, control them or at least minimize their negative impact.

Four themes

The four main themes of this book are:

1. Do the doable. Is there time enough to do everything you need to do and want to do? Clearly the answer is no. Therefore, the first and most important premise you must accept — if you are ever going to manage your time wisely (and rid yourself of unnecessary guilt) — is that there simply isn't enough time to do everything. Most people say they already understand that. Yet, if you watch their behavior at work, they act as if there is enough time to do everything. Think of the person who works lots of overtime hours on very low-priority projects or tasks. That person believes there is enough time to do everything and, unfortunately, has probably lost the balance in his or her life. Since everything is not doable, getting the right things done is most important. In the chapters that follow, you'll learn how to identify and focus on the things that are both urgent and important in your life.

2. **Control the controllable.** Is everything controllable? No. Are other people controllable? No. For that matter, are all people reasonable? No. But most people are trainable. You can often gently persuade them to work better and more closely with you as a time management partner. Later in the book, you'll learn how to gain control of the things in life that are controllable.

3. **Get the right things done.** There are some things you will initially put on your to-do list that will ultimately deserve every bit of procrastination you can give them. Why? Because they will never be urgent enough and important enough for you to give of your time. If you concentrate on getting the right things done, you can live your life without unnecessary guilt. You'll learn how in this book.

4. **Be nice to yourself.** Most of us spend the lion's share of our time responding to the needs and demands of others. There is precious little time left to deal with our own needs. Excellent time management will allow you to reserve more time for the important things in your life. The techniques you'll learn in this book will give you the power to treat yourself to some time of your own.

So let's get started.

1 MAINTAINING BALANCE
How to live your life deliberately

Many — if not most — people are living their lives by accident. How's that for a brash statement? After presenting more than a thousand seminars on five continents to successful professionals like you, I feel justified in making that judgment. Are we stupid, uninterested, careless? Absolutely not. But we do get swept up and carried along by momentum: the momentum of career, the momentum of family, the momentum of spiritual life, even the momentum of success. And if we're not careful, we end up inadvertently right where we don't want to be. In my previous career, for example, my next promotion was a sure thing. My career momentum was exciting and emotionally gratifying ... but ultimately it was leading me toward a destination I did not want. Fortunately, I realized how that promotion would harm the balance in my life. I was able to see how my career momentum would get in the way of the time, effort and attention I wanted to devote to my family. I wasn't willing to accept the imbalance that would result from that promotion. Instead, I deliberately chose another plan. My objective in this chapter and the next is to help you live *your* life on purpose — not by accident — so that you end up where you want to be instead of somewhere else.

Effective time management is not about trying to stuff 32 hours of intense work and frantic activity into a 24-hour day. It's about prioritizing. It's about discovering and then focusing on what is most important. The truth is, time has no *intrinsic* value. For much of the world, time is simply time. Yet in our society, we have grossly inflated time's value. For us, time is money. Time is precious. But only because we're unwilling to narrow our sights and accept limitations. Effective time management, then, is not so much about getting more done, but about getting *the right things done*. Let's start by uncovering what the right things are.

A new look at goal setting

Have you ever tried to set goals? Who hasn't? You know the process: You determine what you want to accomplish (a bigger income, a smaller waistline, more people reporting to you, fewer debts) and *when* you want to accomplish this. You determine what it is you want, how long it will take to get it, and, most important, the steps you must take to get from here to there. Does it work? Ninety-eight people out of every hundred in my seminars say no. Even though these people have not experienced success with goal setting, they have all had another very peculiar thing in common: These same people are very specific about stating where they *didn't* want to end up. They say things like, "I wish I had done this, that or the other thing." Their "I wish I hads" are always very clear and specific. And that's when I hit on the idea I call indirect goal setting. In a nutshell, it doesn't really matter how we reach goals (the "steps"), as long as we can identify desired end points. Simply stated, knowing what we don't want to accomplish is every bit as important as knowing what we *do* hope to achieve. If we can identify potential "I-wish-I-hads," we'll end up closer to where we want to be on purpose, instead of exactly where we didn't want to be by accident.

Prioritizing the demands on your time

Now it's time to get down to work. Figure 1 lists nine broad categories that require time and attention in our lives. We allocate time to socializing, to maintaining health, to family activity and so on. In the exercise that follows, you may be tempted to combine some of the nine categories, but I urge you to resist the temptation at the risk of losing important insights about the demands on your time.

Go down the list in Figure 1 and cross out any categories that are not particularly meaningful, significant or important to you at this point in your life. Bear in mind that what you deem important may change over time. What's most important now may end up less important later, and vice versa. Some categories may, in theory, seem important to you, while in reality you have no time or attention to give them. Cross those off, too. Be careful about what you leave on your list. Don't leave a category in place because you think someone expects you to. This is your list. This is your life. Know that you must eliminate some of the categories. Here's why: Beginning today, you will make a commitment to devote an appropriate amount of time and energy to each category left on your list. No excuses.

Take a look at your list. Are you happy with it? You now have a list of time-demanding categories that are important, meaningful and significant to you. Now, you must be willing to give them the time they deserve. It's perfectly okay to divide your time unevenly among the categories that remain on your list. But remember, the key here is your willingness — your commitment — to give each category the time it deserves.

Today I am 95 — avoiding "I-wish-I-hads"

From studying the nine categories in Figure 1 and eliminating the ones you are unable or unwilling to give time to,

Figure 1

Where is your time spent? Nine categories

Social

Health/Fitness

Career

Education

Family

Spiritual

Personal

Wealth

Leisure

you've gained some useful information. Now, let's put that information to even better use, with the help of a visualization exercise. Immediately below the title of Figure 1, write the words, "Today I am 95." In parentheses, enter your current age.

What's the difference between your current age and 95? That's all the time you have left to avoid any "I wish I hads" and to achieve the balance you want in your life.

Now, picture yourself at age 95. Your family has just thrown a 95th birthday shindig for you. You have just eaten your single cupcake with a single candle on top. After the party, you go out onto the front porch. You put a sweater around your shoulders to keep off the night air. You sit down in the rocking chair on the porch and you rock for a while, forward and backward, forward and backward. You hear the creaking, and you don't know if it is the chair or if it's you.

You begin thinking about your life. For the most part, you feel satisfied. But as you look down by your feet, you find a basket filled with slips of paper the size of chinese cookie fortunes. On each slip of paper is a statement beginning with the words, "I wish I had ..." What do they say?

Take a few minutes now to jot down all the "I wish I hads" you would find in your basket. How do they fit into the categories you kept on your list in Figure 1? Do your "I wish I hads" relate mainly to a single category — career, for instance — or are they spread among several categories? Spend some time arranging your "I wish I hads" within the categories you left on your list. By doing so, you'll be able to see exactly where you want to spend more of your time. This visualization exercise is another critical step in determining where your time priorities lie. Take a look at the completed worksheet in Figure 2. This sample shows some possible "I wish I hads" from the visualization exercise and groups them under some of the nine time-demanding categories.

Figure 2

Where is your time spent? Nine categories

Social

I wish I had spent more time with my friends.

I wish I had spent more time developing new friendships.

Health/Fitness

Career

I wish I had opened that bookstore I always wanted
to have.

I wish I had streamlined the organizational structure of
our company.

Education

I wish I had gone back to school and gotten my degree.

I wish I had gone back to school and gotten a second
degree, or possibly a master's or doctorate.

Family

I wish I had spent more time with my kids.

I wish I had spent more time with my spouse.

Spiritual

I wish I had given more time to my spiritual life.

Personal

I wish I had had more time for me, just to go out in the
backyard, lie down on the grass and watch the clouds
go by.

Wealth

Leisure

I wish I had had more time for my hobbies.

I hope you appreciate the power of what you have just done. You prioritized some of the competing demands on your time (the nine categories) and made a "sanity check" on how you are currently honoring those priorities (the "I wish I hads" visualization). Some people live their entire lives without ever having done what you just did. You now have the opportunity to minimize the number of "I wish I hads" that end up in your basket. Later on, I will describe how you can tie this information into your time management system so that achieving your goals becomes a reality.

A final comment on the "I wish I hads" exercise before we continue: As you visualize your list of "I wish I hads" at age 95, you may discover one or two which are *already* out of your power to remedy. For instance, "I wish I had spent more time with my kids" may appear in your imaginary basket. But, in reality, your children are already grown and out of the house, so there is nothing you can do now to recapture the lost time. Don't let this discourage you. The visualization exercise can't possibly prevent every single "I wish I had" from landing in your basket. The goal is to prevent as many as possible. And even if it's already too late to remedy the regret completely, look for ways to minimize the "I wish I had" or keep it from worsening. For instance, maybe two children are grown and gone, but one child is still living at home. Use the insight you gained from your visualization to devote more time to the son or daughter who still lives at home. And look for creative ways to devote time and attention — it doesn't have to be in person — to the kids who've left the nest. Now you have your list of potential "I wish I hads." You have a clear picture of how you want to spend your time to prevent them. The next step is to rank them in the order you wish to work on them. As your priorities become clearer, you'll decide just how much time you're willing to invest to keep each potential "I wish I had" from becoming a reality.

Making trade-offs ... instead of scrambling for more time

If you now accept that most of us are living our lives by accident, rather than making deliberate choices, it follows that any trade-offs we make in the time we devote to important aspects of our lives is also done by accident. Our trade-offs are often made unconsciously, without our full awareness. It's time to change that. Because the give-and-take of investing your time is far too important to be left to chance. Fortunately, there is a tool to help you become more aware of — and deliberate about — how you make trade-offs between the constantly shifting demands on your time. I call it the "pie chart."

The pie chart

Return for a moment to the categories you left on your list in Figure 1. How many were there? Now, divide the "pie" in Figure 3 into that number of wedges. Initially, all your pie's wedges will have equal size, but later you'll want to redraw the pie so each wedge reflects the amount of time you're committed to giving each category. Remember to label each wedge with the category headings remaining on your list in Figure 1. Your completed pie might look something like this one in figure 3a.

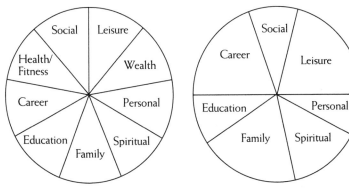

Figure 3: The pie chart   *Figure 3a: Completed pie chart*

Notice that all nine categories aren't necessarily represented. The number of slices and the size of those slices will be determined by where (what category) your "I wish I hads" land and how many land in a given category. Notice how the Family wedge in this example is much larger than the Social wedge, indicating more "family" oriented "I wish I hads" appeared in this basket.

Now that you've divided your pie, it's time to return to the concept of trade-offs. Let's say you want to enlarge the Family wedge of your pie to spend more time with your kids. Then clearly, one or more of the other wedges must get smaller. Remember, your goal is to be as deliberate as possible about which other piece or pieces of your pie will shrink. Don't let it happen by accident.

Before reallocating your time — making trade-offs — you must have a clear picture of how your pie looks right now. The size of the wedges as they are now will lead to a basket full of "I wish I hads." Preventing "I wish I hads" is as simple as slicing your pie differently.

Here's an example from my own life. Like so many others, I wanted to enlarge the Family wedge in my pie. The first wedge I analyzed was Career. I quickly realized that a lot of the time I should have spent with my two oldest boys went into my career. I was working a lot of overtime — staying late, bringing work home and returning to the office on weekends. I assumed all of that overtime was essential. Only when I forced myself to do a time log did I realize how wrong I was. I logged all my working hours, plus I assigned priority codes to what I was working on. Wow! What a wake-up call. I discovered that my problem wasn't a heavy workload. My problem was not fully accepting — mentally and emotionally — the fact that there isn't enough time to do everything. Now I know better. I also discovered that I was working countless overtime hours on extremely low-priority projects and tasks.

At that point, I made an immediate decision, one that I have never regretted. I recommend you make the same decision if you are working a lot of overtime or are tempted to do so in the future. Commit to never again spending overtime hours on low-priority tasks.

That deliberate decision alone significantly shrunk the Career wedge in my pie, allowing me to add time to Family. As we near the end of this century and enter the next, there will be increased pressures on all of us to work longer hours. With that in mind, let me politely and professionally challenge you. The next time you think you ought to work overtime to complete a low-priority task, look at your "Pie." Place your index finger on the wedge you are willing to sacrifice, in whole or in part, to complete that low- priority task. What you see should shake you right off the treadmill and force you to reconsider your priorities.

What if taking time from one wedge to add to another isn't enough? Keep right on re-slicing your pie. In my case, I took a hard look at my Personal wedge. This generated another wake-up call. I realized I was guilty of being a perfectionist about things that weren't really important. Misplaced perfectionism is the plague of any time management system. Consider this: The last 10% of the trip to perfection, in your professional and personal life, costs as much in time, effort and other resources as the first 90%. With that in mind, we need to ask ourselves constantly if that final 10% is truly worthwhile. In other words, are we doing the right things right?

Let me give you an example of what I mean. As a perfectionist, if I were painting a bedroom in our home, sooner or later you would find me inside the closet, up above the shelf at the top inside corner where the ceiling meets the two walls. I'd be scrunched up there like Michelangelo in the Sistine Chapel, using an artist's brush, trying to paint a perfect line between the ceiling and the walls. I would have been better off just dropping down a rung or two on the ladder, taking a large brush with paint on it and quickly painting what could loosely approximate a straight line up in that top inside corner of the closet. The truth is, there will probably never be another person in the world who will ever know whether the paint line between the ceiling and the wall was perfect.

Let's assume I mustered the courage to save time by using the large brush and simply approximating a straight line. Although no one else is ever likely to know if that line was perfect or not, if you are a perfectionist, you're already thinking, "Yes, Dick, but *you'll* know. And knowing that it isn't straight will eventually drive you crazy."

Here's an effective way to keep less-than-perfect results from driving the perfectionist in you crazy. Make contracts with yourself about those things that don't need to be perfect. In other words, give yourself permission to be imperfect. Let me return to the bedroom closet. Let's assume I do take the larger brush and quickly paint a less-than-perfectly-straight line between the ceiling and the wall. Next I need to make a contract with myself that if that uneven line is still bothering me a week later, I will pull out all my painting materials again, return to the closet, and fix that uneven line. Know what? It'll never happen. By next week I'll have so many other demands on my time that I won't recall whether I even painted a line, let alone whether it was straight or not.

Perfectionism can derail larger projects too. I got another wake-up call when I was doing some remodeling work in a small bathroom off of the master bedroom in our home. Even though I was only doing some wallpapering, caulking and painting, the project seemed to be taking forever. My perfectionism kept progress moving at a snail's pace. Sometimes I would redo perfectly acceptable work because it wasn't perfect. Then one day I stopped myself and asked, "Dick, what's going on here?" I knew. Perfectionism was coming up right out of my socks and strangling me. And I realized that wallpaper seams were taking priority over my son's Little League games.

So, I decided to whip through the rest of the project as quickly as I could, while at the same time giving myself permission to be imperfect. As I worked, I felt a tremendous burden lifting from my shoulders and I really started cooking. But once again, I needed to make a contract with myself to prevent the perfectionist tendency from controlling me. So I pulled out my calendar and made an appointment with myself to check my work 90 days later. I promised myself that when the 90th day arrived, I would go back into that bathroom and fix or redo anything that was still bothering me. Within two or three days, I knew I was already "home free." Not surprisingly, by the 90th day not one thing about the remodeling work looked amiss. Why? Because time heals perfectionism.

Of course, the process of controlling misplaced perfectionism applies equally in your professional life. If you find yourself taking far too much time completing a minor administrative report, complete the report as quickly as you can, and don't worry about being perfect. I'm not suggesting you fudge facts or miscalculate numbers. I'm simply recommending you let go of the fancy computer graphics, or eliminate time you spend making the five-cent report look like a 10-dollar document. Make a contract with yourself to review and "fix" the report at the end of the next working day if you are still concerned about any imperfections. By the end of the next workday, you will have so many other crocodiles nipping at your heels that nothing could make you look at that report again.

Remember, being perfect about a task that demands and deserves perfection is one thing. But not every task does. In short, don't sweat the small stuff. As you learn to keep perfectionism in check, you'll not only have more time for higher priorities, but you'll be treating yourself better — being nicer to yourself — in the process.

No time like the present

When should you start working to eliminate your "I wish I hads"? The answer is simple: right now. It goes without saying that potential "I wish I hads" will surface before you are

95. In fact, some may already exist. Again, the trick is to keep more from accumulating in your imaginary basket. Stating "I wish I had opened a bookstore" doesn't mean that I should open a bookstore when I'm 94. Rather, it says I should develop a plan right now for preventing myself from ending up with that "I wish I had."

Identifying exactly where you want to be spending your time and preventing potential "I wish I hads" is, of course, a long-term process. It also requires long-term goal setting. But there's nothing wrong with an entrepreneur or manager using the visualization exercise in this chapter for short-term tasks and projects. Instead of imagining you're 95, imagine only 90 days have passed. Ninety days from now, if you keep doing what you're doing now and allocating your time the way you're allocating it now, what professional or career "I wish I hads" could you end up with? Visualize 90 days out. Visualize six months in the future. Make the time period whatever you want it to be. The important thing is to ask the question, "If I keep investing my time as I'm investing it now, what regrets will I have?"

Beating the vicious circle of stress

As we already established, when you give too much of your time to only one slice of your pie, you lose balance in your life. If you lose balance in your life, what happens to your stress level? It goes sky high, doesn't it? And what happens when your stress level goes sky high? You start scurrying around, flitting from one thing to another — trying to do everything instead of working by priorities and getting the right things done. It's as futile as trying to herd squirrels. And as your stress level soars, you can actually become the squirrel. You start scampering to work on those things that give you closure, whether or not they are important. You tend to work on tasks that are quick, interesting or fun regardless of their importance. And what doesn't get done in the process? The

highest-priority projects and tasks. Your scampering and scurrying backfire. With high-priority tasks left undone, stress
continues to soar. The more stress, the less accomplished. It's
an unending cycle. The good news is, with the tools you've
gained in this chapter, you'll be well on your way to beating it.

Actions to take now

1. Accept a fundamental fact: No one has enough time
   to do everything.

2. Evaluate and re-evaluate where — exactly — you want
   to be spending your time. What are your time-invest-
   ment priorities?

3. Approximately every six months, repeat the visualization exercise to update potential "I wish I hads" and
   prevent them.

4. Re-evaluate the time allocation trade-offs you are making in your life.

2 GOAL SETTING
How to prioritize your actions

Converting dreams to goals

For most people, goal setting never goes beyond dreaming. We all have vague aspirations — but as nice as they are, they are not goals. Few of us take time to write out our goals, let alone break them into a format that will help us achieve them. In this chapter, we're going to explore how to turn dreams into specific goals and learn a goal-setting process that will keep your "I wish I hads" from landing in your basket.

Figure 4 is a goal-setting framework designed to answer four simple questions: what, why, how and when.

Let me take a moment to explain each of these four questions and why answering them is critical to successful goal setting.

1. What? (Statement of Objective)

The objective is what you want to achieve. Here's another way to look at it: Objectives are the actions you will take to prevent "I wish I hads" from occurring. You've already spent the time and effort to identify your "I wish I hads," so it makes good sense to capitalize on that. Now write down what you intend to do to prevent the "I wish I had" from landing in your

Figure 4

Setting goals

What? (statement of objective)

Why? (your reasons)

How? (actions required)

When? (start/completion dates)

basket. For example, to prevent "I wish I had spent more time with my family," your objective will be, "I will spend two additional hours of quality time with each child per week."

2. Why? (What's in It for Me?)

Here, list your reasons for wanting to achieve the stated objective. You may be tempted to skip this step because the reasons behind your objective seem self-evident. Even so, put them in writing! In written form, they will motivate you to achieve your stated objectives. You should review these reasons frequently. Putting them in writing and keeping them in front of you is the best way to do that. When you have recorded all your reasons in the "why" step, you will notice something interesting. Nearly every reason will be terribly, terribly selfish — and that's great! People rarely act in other people's interests. Instead, most of our actions are motivated by self-interest. We do things to benefit ourselves. So, the more selfish the better, because you're more likely to meet your objectives when there's something in it for you. For instance, if your objective is to spend more time with your kids, your reasons might include: "I will decrease the guilt I feel for depriving them of my time and attention." Or, "I will enjoy the peace of mind that will come from knowing more about them as well as how and where they spend their time."

3. How? (Actions Required)

This third step is critically important to achieving your goals. Make no assumptions. List every single step or action you must take to prevent your "I wish I had" from occurring. Be as specific as possible. In our example, your "how" section might include statements like, "I will eat breakfast with my son three mornings each week." Or, "I will jog with my daughter every other day."

4. When? (Start/Completion Dates)

Write down the start date for the first action you want to take in the "how" section above. Then write down your completion date, if you can reasonably determine what it should be. Occasionally, you won't know your final completion date until you have completed at least some of the actions in the "how" section.

Set achievable goals

Follow the "what, why, how and when" formula, and you'll end up with specific and measurable goals. But a worthwhile goal should also be achievable. It's important that you push yourself, but you should also be realistic. Realistic means that you should have at least an 80–90% chance of successfully achieving the goal. Anything less than that means you're probably setting yourself up to fail. A 100% chance of achieving your goal may mean that you're being too easy on yourself. There's another benefit to having achievable goals: The more realistic they are, the more committed you'll be to your goals, and the less likely it is that others will try to recruit you to help them achieve their goals.

Make them relevant

Another characteristic of a worthwhile goal is relevance. Make sure your goal pertains to what you ought to be doing. Don't set a career goal for yourself which runs counter to the goals of your organization. If you do, you're going to get yourself into a lot of trouble. Specific, measurable, achievable and relevant — those are the guidelines for creating worthwhile goals.

Goal versus wish

Have you ever made a New Year's resolution? How did you fare? Did you lose three pounds ... only to gain five back? Did you sign up for a two-day computer course ... and then drop out after the first day? It's a laugh, isn't it? Let's analyze New Year's resolutions according to our goals format. Did you know your objective — what you wanted to do? Yes. Did you know why you wanted to do it? Yes, you'd known the reasons for a long time. Did you know when you wanted to start? Of course, New Year's Day. What was the problem? Why didn't you keep your New Year's resolution? Because you didn't have the fourth component of a well-stated goal — the "how." In other words, you had no specific game plan for achieving your New Year's resolution. You didn't have a goal. You had a wish. Knowing *how* to take action transforms wishes into goals.

To understand the power of the goal-setting format I've recommended to you, next New Year's Eve, set only two resolutions. The reason? Most New Year's resolutions have to do with deeply embedded habits that are not easily changed. So never create more than two New Year's resolutions. Then work on those two, one at a time. The name of the game is not quantity, it's actually achieving your goal. Replace one bad habit with a new behavior, then move on to your second New Year's resolution.

I'd like to share a personal example of how powerful the goal-setting format can be.

I'm not proud of this, but I was a smoker for 37 years. I tried to quit many times but consistently failed. Whenever I tried, I just assumed that all a person had to do to quit smoking was just stop buying cigarettes. Not true.

It wasn't until I prepared a goal sheet for quitting that I realized what my problem had been. The "how" step was the key. It told me that it's not just a matter of not buying cigarettes, it's a matter of changing the deeply embedded habits that are tied to a cigarette in one's hand or in one's mouth. For example, a common pattern for smokers is to eat a very nice dinner, follow it with dessert, a cup of coffee or two and some of the best tasting cigarettes of the day. The "how" step of the goal setting format showed me that, if I was ever going to stop smoking, I would have to finish my main meal, skip dessert and coffee, get up from the table and get busy doing something else which would lessen my craving for an after-dinner cigarette.

Whether it's quitting smoking, going on a diet, learning to save more money or starting an exercise program, the goal-setting format I've presented in this chapter will put you on a path to success rather than doom you to failure.

Prioritize your objectives

As I said in Chapter 1, prioritizing your objectives is important. You have a couple of options for prioritizing: You can 1) develop all your objectives at once, then stack them in the order you'll want to work on them, or 2) you can prepare a goal sheet for just those objectives you can reasonably accommodate in the near future. The choice is yours.

I've shared a lot of information in this chapter regarding the goal-setting process. Now a concrete example is in order to solidify this process in your mind. So here it goes:

Example: "I wish I had achieved a position of supervisor."

Assume one of the slips in my basket at age 95 says, "I wish I had achieved a position of supervisor" (or manager or leader within my company or organization). What am I willing to do right now to prevent that "I wish I had"? Before I spell out how I could become a supervisor, I have to know the why. Why do I want to do this in the first place? Here are my answers: I will have greater responsibility. I will have more challenge in my job. I want to have a greater sense of pride in my work. I want to feel that I'm contributing something. I want to feel that I'm giving something back. I want to feel like I'm helping other people in a supervisory or management function. I want to be in a position to help others become not just as good as they thought they could be, but far better than they ever dreamed they could be.

When do I want to start? I want to start right now. And I'll do that by finding out how to stay on top of supervisory positions that are opening and might be right for me. What's my outside completion date? Within one year from today I will be in a leadership, management or supervisory position. How am I going to do that? One of the first things I'm going to do is get support from my home environment by telling my spouse and the rest of my family what I'm trying to achieve. I'm also going to tell my boss, so I can get support at work. Announcing your goals to others (going public) will generate the added support you need to be successful in achieving your goal.

In addition to announcing my goal, I'm going to find a community college or a university where I can pick up a management theory course. I'm going to look for a high-quality seminar on basic supervisory skills. And I'm going to take on every special project I can find where I'll have leadership opportunities. At every meeting I attend, I'm going to raise my hand and volunteer for projects. I'm going to show my initiative, creativity and innovation. I'm going to accept as many new tasks and projects as I can. Whenever possible, I'm also going to volunteer to present the results of ad hoc committees, task groups and other committee efforts to senior management. Doing so will give me added visibility.

Again, the whole point of the "how" step is to write down every specific action you'll need to take to achieve your goal, regardless of whether that goal applies to your professional or your personal life, to the near term or the long term.

Consider just one of your goals. Now that you know what actions you need to take to achieve your objective (the "how") and have all the required actions listed under the "how" step, how can you tie those actions into your time management system? In order of priority, those actions should flow to your to-do list (I will explain the to-do list in Chapter 3). Since all those actions have to do with important aspects of your life, are they going to have a high or low priority? High. And because they have a high priority, they stand a very good chance of making it from your to-do list to your "daily plans" (we'll cover "daily plans" in Chapter 4) for accomplishment.

Here's my challenge to you. For the rest of your life, beginning tomorrow, make sure every daily plan you create contains at least one action for preventing an "I wish I had" from occurring in your life. Start off with one action per day and let the momentum of success build. In no time, you will be working on two or three "I wish I had" prevention actions each day.

Let's take a look at several examples that demonstrate the power of "I wish I had" goal setting. I was in Atlanta, Georgia, presenting a full-day time management seminar. We covered the goal-setting part of the program just before lunch. As we broke, a young woman came up to me and said, "Boy, I'm glad we did this." And I said, "Why?" "Because as I was looking at the family aspect of my life," she said, "I realized that I didn't want to end up being 95 years old having had only one son." She continued, "I just decided to have another baby."

Her husband picked her up from the seminar that afternoon. When he arrived, she introduced him to me. Then she turned to him and made her announcement. Trust me, I cannot adequately describe how he looked at me. But as I looked into his eyes, I realized something: Here were two loving, intimate, caring people who wanted exactly the same thing and had never talked about it. The point is, you should share your goals with those who mean the most to you. In so doing, you will identify common goals and you can mutually support each other.

A second example comes from another time management seminar I was conducting in Fort Collins, Colorado. There were 250 people in the room. At noon, 249 people got up and left for lunch. One gentlemen, sitting way in the back, didn't leave with the others. I assumed he was going to skip lunch. So I proceeded to set up my charts and get ready for the afternoon session. Out of my peripheral vision, I noticed the man moving toward me. So I looked up to address him. I was shocked to see two very large tears coming down his cheeks.

In a very shaky voice, he said, "Dick, I want to apologize for being out of control. I've been struggling for the entire

35 minutes we've been doing this exercise. When I looked up at your 'Balance in Your Life' chart, the family category was like a giant flashing neon sign — family, family, family. I realized that I don't have one. Fifteen years ago my father married my stepmother and we have not spoken a word to each other since. In doing the exercise, I realized I am not willing to go through the rest of my life without a family, and I wanted you to know that when I leave this seminar today, the very first thing I'm going to do is call my dad."

Powerful stuff! This was a significant reversal of the decision this man made some 15 years ago. Why did it happen? For just a few minutes, he got off the treadmill of life and took a hard look at what was important to him.

A third example occurred while I was presenting a seminar in Scotland. A British gentleman told me that the "I wish I had" exercise had guided him back to reality. He told me how he used to play a round of golf once a month, then it was twice a month, then it was every Saturday and Sunday. Eventually, he was playing every holiday as well, and ultimately he stopped to play nine holes three times a week on his way home from work. Talk about being swept up by momentum! He said, "I just realized something. I have a 13-year-old son. I don't have a clue who he really is. I don't know what he thinks, what his worries or concerns or problems are, how he feels about those around him, or what he needs from me. I just decided that I'm going back to playing golf two days a month and I'm going to go find out who my son is." I don't know about you, but I think this is a fellow who is finally getting his priorities straight.

What if your goals are incompatible with those of people close to you?

Before turning to the next chapter, let's consider an important question about goal setting. What if the actions you want to take to prevent an "I wish I had" from occurring in your life are incompatible with the needs of others who are close to you?

To prevent conflicts and incompatibilities with those who are important to you, it's very important for you to go through the "I wish I had" exercise with them. After each of you have identified your "I wish I hads" and have created your goal sheets, share your goals with each other, especially your "how" steps. What you may find is that part of your action plan to prevent one of your "I wish I hads" from occurring is diametrically opposed to the action plan of the other person. For example, you're going to school three nights a week to work on an "I wish I had" pertaining to education. But then, you look at your partner's "I wish I had" and it says, "I want to spend more time with you, particularly evenings." In this instance, your desires are in conflict with each other, and you will need to negotiate a solution so each of you can achieve at least a portion of what you want.

Actions to take now

1. Identify short-term (up to 90 days) and long-term (more than 90 days) "I wish I had" prevention objectives.

2. Set goals by answering four questions: What? Why? How? and When?

3. Make sure your goals are specific, measurable, achievable and relevant.

4. Set goals, don't make wishes.

5. Prioritize your objectives and complete a goal sheet for each one.

6. Make sure your goals are compatible with the goals of others who are close to you. Ask those who are close to you to go through the "I wish I had" visualization exercise with you.

3 ORGANIZING AND PRIORITIZING
How to record and rank your daily tasks

Now that you've learned how to set specific, measurable, achievable and relevant goals, it's time to get organized, so you can accomplish those goals. In this chapter, I'll explain how to create a "to-do" list that saves more time than it takes to keep. I'll also tell you where to look for items that should end up on your to-do list, and the best way to prioritize them. Then, in Chapter 4, I will provide you with an effective format for your to-do list.

What is a to-do list?

A to-do list is a running, "scratch-'n'-carry" list of tasks, activities and projects that you may one day want to accomplish. Notice the not-so-subtle suggestion: You may choose to leave items from a to-do list undone. As I hinted in the Introduction, not everything you initially place on your to-do list will ultimately get done. The key is to get the right things done, and leave the things that aren't important undone.

It's a dirty job

There's a reality you should know about to-do lists: They get messy. Enter items on your to-do list, and when their degree of importance gets high enough, move them to your "daily plan" and cross them off your to-do list. As a result, your to-do list will start looking messy. You may be tempted to rewrite it and make it look neater.

Let me be blunt: Rewriting a to-do list for the sake of being neat is a total waste of time. Remember what a time-thief perfectionism can be. To-do lists are meant to be messy. In fact, when you have filled up the front and back of the first page of your to-do list, grab another page. Staple it to the first, and keep going. You may eventually add a third page and a fourth. Don't let length intimidate you. Again, you may choose to leave items from a to-do list undone.

After some time has passed, consider all the tasks that were left undone on the first page of your to-do list. Notice that with the passage of time, they did not upgrade in priority or importance and therefore they did not warrant your attention. At that point, tear off page one and throw it away. Whatever is left on page one is probably never going to get done. If you can't force yourself to throw it away, reserve a desk drawer as a "slush" file. Put page one in there and close the drawer quickly. If any of the uncompleted items raise their ugly heads again, you'll know where that to-do page is and you can quickly retrieve it. Realistically, it's not going to happen.

Sources of to-do list items

Four primary sources generate items for most of our to-do lists. They include:

Boss-imposed tasks

The first and probably the most important source of to-do list tasks is your boss. Have you ever worked for a boss who assigned top priority to every task he or she gave you? In that situation, it's up to you to rank the tasks according to their relative priority. Today's hectic, pressured work pace has forced many bosses to abdicate the responsibility of helping employees prioritize their workloads. When you try to guess your boss's true priorities, sometimes you'll be right and sometimes you'll be wrong. When you're wrong, the boss will probably get upset with you — and that's not fair. After all, bosses get paid to let you know the organization's true priorities. However, though it might not be fair, it is reality for most of us, so you need a tool to help you reinvolve your boss in helping set priorities.

Consider using something I like to call the "Boss Attack List." No, it is not a list of who you're going to attack. It's simply a list of the tasks your boss has given you to do, prioritized in the sequence you plan to attack them. This is separate from your to-do list.

Keep your Boss Attack List close at hand. The next time your boss comes by and says, "Here's another top-priority task I want you to work on," pull out your list, hand it to your boss and say, "I'll be happy to work on that for you. By the way, these are the other tasks you've given me, and that's the order in which I plan to attack them unless you change it. Where do you see this additional task fitting in?" The boss may say something like, "Put it between numbers three and four." Don't forget to say thank-you, because your boss's involvement in the process will take a lot of pressure off you.

On the other hand, if your boss responds with, "You figure it out," then your boss is resisting getting reinvolved. It might be that your boss hasn't actually thought about or figured out each job's relative priority. Don't give up — at least not right away. Try to reinvolve your boss several times before abandoning your Boss Attack List. If your boss continues to resist, discard the Boss Attack List because you certainly don't want your boss to get so uncomfortable that he or she will "free up your future." You owe it to yourself, though, to give the Boss Attack List a fair try.

Years ago, I worked with a guy named Bob who got his boss reinvolved in the prioritizing process by using the Attack List technique. After a week of asking his boss to help prioritize items on his list, he simply taped his list to the outside of his cubicle. Each subsequent time the boss came by to assign another task, he would pause outside the cubicle, look over the list, then approach Bob and say something like, "Put this one between numbers two and three." Bob had succeeded in reinvolving his boss in the prioritizing process.

System-imposed tasks

A second source of to-do list items is system-imposed activities. These are tasks you do on a regular basis. They are always done in the same way. Examples include routine requirements to prepare reports, produce computer printouts, write letters or memos, and so forth. If I asked you how urgent and important that bi-weekly sales report you prepare is, you'd probably say, "Not very." Do you still have to prepare it? Yes. Just remember the time you spend dealing with system-imposed activities detracts from the time you'll have to spend on the to-do list items that you want to work on. System-imposed activities are one of three factors that will comprise the "uncontrollable" time in your workday. I will discuss uncontrollable time in detail in the next chapter.

Subordinate-imposed tasks

A third source of items that end up on your to-do list is subordinate-imposed tasks. These are all the things your peers, and those you supervise, ask you to do. Some of these tasks are legitimate; many others result from a pitfall known as reverse delegation. Here's how it works: If you supervise or manage other people, you delegate projects and tasks to them. But you've probably found that sometimes when you delegate a task to a person on your team, somehow it ends up back on *your* to-do list. You delegated the task to Barbara, for example, and she ran into some difficulty accomplishing it. So she brought it back to you hoping you would take back both the task and the problem.

Because you were headed for a meeting when Barbara

intercepted you for help, you probably said something like, "Excuse me, Barbara, but I'm late for a meeting. Tell you what," then you muttered the five deadly words, "let me look into it." The task is now back on your to-do list, and you volunteered to put it there. To avoid reverse delegation, try your best never to say "let me look into it" when someone tries to throw a task back in your lap. In the next chapter, I'll share three questions you need to ask that will keep the ball in the other person's court and help you control reverse delegation. These questions will also help your peers and subordinates grow and develop into more competent professionals.

Self-imposed tasks

The fourth source of to-do list items is self-imposed goals and activities. Self-imposed goals and activities are the things you want to do just for you. Examples might include reading a journal article or attending a training seminar. If, however, you take time for boss-imposed tasks, system-imposed activities and subordinate-imposed actions, how much time is usually left for self-imposed goals and activities? Almost none. Notice who comes out at the bottom of the heap. You deserve better than that. As you learn to manage your time more effectively, you'll be able to increase the time you spend on self-imposed tasks.

At this point, you know what an effective to-do list should look like and where to-do list items come from. Also, we've already established that not everything initially placed on your to-do list will get done. So to get the right things done, you need to consider some prioritizing concepts and tools.

The Pareto Principle (80/20 rule)

Pareto was a 16th-century economist who said that in any set of items, 20% of the items account for 80% of the set's entire value. The other 80% of the items in the set take a great deal of time, energy and resources, but account for only 20% of the set's total value.

Here are some examples of the Pareto Principle at work:

- In sales, it is often true that 20% of a firm's customers generate 80% of the company's gross income.

- If an employee has 10 responsibilities, two of those account for 80% of the person's value to the organization.

- Furthermore, an employee loses visibility and credibility if he or she gets trapped into working on the 80% of the assigned responsibilities that account for only 20% of the person's value to the organization.

- Frequently 80% of what's accomplished in a meeting is generated by only 20% of the people at the meeting.

The Pareto Principle is sometimes referred to as the concept of the critical few (the 20%) and the trivial many (the 80%). It's a concept that offers us a theoretical framework for prioritizing our efforts.

The priority matrix

The Pareto Principle gives you a theory. Now you need a system. This priority matrix will help you take a look at priority for each item on your to-do list and ultimately on your daily plans. The horizontal axis of the matrix ranks the relative importance of a task, from high importance on the left to low importance on the right. The vertical axis ranks the relative urgency of a task, from high urgency at the top to low urgency on the bottom. The priority matrix is divided into four quadrants which allow you to assess a task's relative importance and urgency in combination. Every task on your to-do list will fit into one of the four quadrants.

Figure 5

	High	Importance	Low

Quadrant diagram:
- **1** Do it now (High Urgency, High Importance)
- **3** Typical interruptions (High Urgency, Low Importance)
- **2** Mid- to long-range planning (Low Urgency, High Importance)
- **4** Trivia (Low Urgency, Low Importance)

Quadrant One — Do it now!

Placing a to-do list item in Quadrant One means it is both highly important and highly urgent, so you need to do it right away. Quadrant One tasks are do-it-now tasks. For example, you have a major client on the telephone talking to your assistant. The client is extremely upset about the way his account was handled during the last two weeks. He's angry and wants to talk to you, the account representative, right now. Do you take the call? Yes. You want to keep your client and your job, don't you?

Good judgment and common sense, of course, dictate that you should accept the call. The problem with good judgment and common sense in time management is that they don't always function for you when you need them. Other things get in the way such as deeply embedded habits, emotions, "knee-jerk" reactions and so forth. You will be more successful if you rely on objective tools that won't fail you the way good judgment and common sense can. Using effective tools is especially critical when you consider that about 80% of your time-management efforts happen on a subconscious level. As I've already explained, a major objective of time management is increasing your conscious awareness of time-consuming priorities. Again, it's about using your time on purpose — not by accident.

So, let's use the priority matrix in the example, rather than good judgment and common sense, to help us decide if we should accept that irate client's telephone call. What is the call's level of importance? High. What is the level of urgency? High. High importance, high urgency — Quadrant One, "do it now." Accept the call.

Here's another couple of examples. A pipe breaks out in the hallway, and there's half-an-inch of water on the floor. You need to fix the leak. What quadrant are we in? One. You have a major report printing that will give you all the data you need to support your funding requests for the next two years. Suddenly, the computer system crashes. You need to save your data. What quadrant are you in? Again, you are in Quadrant One, the "do it now" quadrant.

Quadrant Two — Mid- and long-range planning

Tasks assigned to Quadrant Two are highly important, but not urgent. When we are faced with a job that's highly important but not urgent, what do we tend to do with it? It's not very pressing, so we usually put a Quadrant Two task off on the side burner. Sometimes we even push it to the back burner.

Typically, Quadrant Two tasks involve mid- and long-range planning. Important? Sure. Is it urgent? No, so we tend to put it off. But beware, tasks in Quadrant Two will become Quadrant One crises if they are ignored indefinitely. Employee training is a good example of a Quadrant Two task. It's important but not urgent. Training is easy to put off. But when you suddenly need better-trained employees, and you don't have them, training becomes an urgent and important task.

Our goal with this prioritizing system is to reduce the number of Quadrant One crises you have to deal with. I don't care how pressed you are for time, as you move through the rest of this decade and into the next century, you need to devote time to mid- and long-range thinking and planning on a regular basis. Why? Because it's the best way to reduce the number of Quadrant One crises you will have to deal with in the future.

How often should you conduct mid- and long-range planning sessions? It depends on the nature of your work and your industry, but most people should have a solid block of time devoted to mid- and long-range planning once a month, once every other month, or at least once a quarter. Mid- and long-range planning is important, not only in your career, but also to your personal and family life.

Quadrant Three — Typical interruptions

Quadrant Three tasks include all the typical interruptions that plague your day. In Quadrant Three, the urgency level is high, but the importance level is low. Another label for Quadrant Three might be "Just as soon as …." Here's why: Have you ever heard yourself saying, "I'm going to start working on that very difficult, complex, boring, major task which is important and urgent — just as soon as I clear up a few of these other loose ends on my desk"? These just-as-soon-as tasks often seem urgent, but they are rarely important. From now on, as soon as your mind says "just as soon as," stop and consider the value of what you're about to work on. The fact is, you are about to embark on something that is not very important, though it might seem urgent. And the trouble with these typical interruptions is that they keep you from doing the more important Quadrant One and Two activities. So watch out for the Quadrant Three "just-as-soon-as" traps.

Here are a few statistics about the typical interruptions that often fit into Quadrant Three. First, on average you are interrupted every six to nine minutes. Second, your average recovery time per interruption is four to five minutes — that's how long it takes to get mentally, physically and emotionally back to where you were before you were interrupted. Combining the numbers — interruptions every six to nine minutes, plus four to five minutes to get back on track — is it any wonder that we go home frustrated and discouraged, and often feeling guilty about not having gotten more done?

Picture this. You are working at your desk. Your office door is open, and a colleague comes down the hall, knocks at the door frame and asks, "Got a minute?" How do we most often respond? We say, "Sure, come on in." The person sits down and begins to tell you about his or her issue. After politely listening for a few minutes, you begin to think, "This is nice, but considering my priorities, I don't have time for this." You see, it's not really the Quadrant One crises that are killing our time management efforts. The culprits are Quadrant Two, Three and Four matters that we handle as if they belonged in Quadrant One.

Businesspeople often deal with routine, low-priority interruptions as if they were actually high-priority (Quadrant One) tasks. I've coined a term to fit that situation: "blurting." My wife, Jackie, made me aware of exactly what blurting is all about. We work together in the same office and sit diagonally across from each other. One day I was working at my desk when Jackie swiveled around in her chair and said, "Dick, do you realize you've driven my productivity down to almost zero?" Reacting with surprise, I said no. "Well," she said, "do you know how many times a day you interrupt me?" I said no. We've been married for more than three decades, and I know her well enough to know when she's upset, so I thought I'd better look into it. For the next 10 days, every time I interrupted her, I wrote down what the interruption was about and

I assigned it a priority matrix code. Boy, what a wake-up call that was. After 10 days of consciously tracking these interruptions, I realized I was guilty of "blurting." Every time anything came into my mind which I thought Jackie might be even remotely interested in, I blurted it out. Because she didn't want to be rude or discourteous, she would respond. So every time I blurted and Jackie responded, regardless of priority, it was an interruption for her. And don't forget, she would also lose four to five minutes in recovery time to get back on track. What also impressed me about recording these interruptions was that 90% of my blurts actually fit into quadrants Two, Three and Four, but I was treating them as if they belonged in Quadrant One. I know you don't want to reduce the amount of communication within your organization or company, but it is critical to create some discipline around the communication process. Ask yourself: Can you really afford to allow others to interrupt you at their whim with nonurgent, nonimportant matters, and can you be allowed to do the same to them?

For a while, I thought I was the only "blurter" around. Then I began to watch what was going on in the organizations that were hiring me for on-site seminars. I became acutely aware that blurting is pervasive. We blurt to our bosses, our bosses blurt to us. We blurt to our peers, customers and employees and they blurt back to us. And pity those poor administrative assistants. They have numerous bosses blurting at them all day long — then one of the bosses usually has the audacity to ask, "Didn't you get that memo typed for me?" A perfectly legitimate response would be: "No, sir, I've been in recovery all day."

All of us need to get blurting under control. Here's a two-step process that will help you get a handle on it and save a minimum of three weeks per year in the process. Better yet, if you share this process with those around you and they use it too, you'll save even more time.

First, put your priority matrix on a 3" x 5" card and place it at the top center of your desk or work area. Don't move it, and don't cover it up. For 30 to 60 days, you need to be able to see it instantly so you can train yourself to think in terms of the priority matrix. The next time you are tempted to blurt, decide which quadrant the interruption fits into. Use the priority matrix to drive into your conscious mind the real value of the interruption. Chances are good it's low.

Second, get yourself what we'll refer to as a "save-up tablet" and keep it close at hand. Here's how you'll use it. Every time you're tempted to "blurt," first look at your priority matrix and place the "blurt" in its proper quadrant. If it's Quadrant One, what should you do? Blurt! It's warranted. The interruption is justified. It's high in importance, high in urgency, Quadrant One. But if it falls into Quadrant Two, Three or Four, it goes on the save-up tablet. Jot down a word or two to identify the matter, along with the person's name to whom it applies. Once or twice a day, get together with your co-workers and discuss all the save-ups on your list.

Initially, you may find that the two-step process *takes* as much time as it *saves*. But not for long. Evaluating potential interruptions in terms of the priority matrix will become automatic, and you'll be on your way to reclaiming weeks of lost time each year. Did you decrease the amount of communication needed within your organization? No. Out of necessity, did you discipline the communication process? Yes. If you consider the resulting decrease in the total number of interruptions per day and the reduction in associated recovery time, then you multiply all of that time saved by more than 240 workdays per year, you're saving a significant amount of time. Chapters 1 and 2 should have helped you determine what to do with at least some of that time saved.

Quadrant Four — Trivia

Quadrant Four is labeled Trivia. That's because it is reserved for tasks that are both low in importance and low in urgency.

Tasks that fall into this category might include: Reading unsolicited promotional materials, rewriting or straightening up your to-do list and tidying up your desk even though your "organized mess" isn't slowing you down. To the left of the four boxes in Figure 5, write vertically down the side, V-A-L-U-E — because value exists in Quadrants One and Two, but there's little value in Quadrants Three and Four. Unfortunately, 60% of the time we spend dealing with Quadrant Three and Four matters and issues is time that should have been spent in Quadrants One and Two. So be ferocious about fighting your way over into Quadrants One and Two. At the same time, try to minimize the time you spend on tasks in Quadrants Three and Four.

Socializing at work

Does socializing at work always belong in Quadrant Four? Not always. Socializing at work can sometimes belong to Quadrant One or Two. Let's assume that I work for Leigh as an administrative assistant and office manager. This morning, Leigh is in her office thinking, "You know, I really don't have a good rapport established with Dick. Our relationship is not at the open, professional level where I would like it to be." So Leigh comes out of her office and deliberately socializes with me for three or four minutes. Her specific objective is to improve our professional relationship. In what quadrant or quadrants is Leigh operating at this point? One or Two, depending on whether Leigh perceives her efforts to improve our working relationship as a short-term or long-term process.

Let me change the scenario. Let's assume that Leigh and I already have great rapport in our professional relationship and she inadvertently or accidently socializes with me for three or four minutes. What quadrant is she in? Four. So the point is, almost nothing in and of itself fits exclusively into any one of the four quadrants. Certain tasks and activities can move from high importance to low importance, and from high urgency to low urgency, depending on the day's objectives.

Let's make sure you understand the priority matrix. If your house is in flames and you need to put out the fire, what quadrant are you in? One. Maybe. It depends on how much you like your house and how much it's insured for. Now, please think about and write down one example of a task, activity or project that you worked on in the past week that fell into each of the four quadrants.

Actions to take now

1. Keep a messy, scratch-'n'-carry to-do list.

2. Maintain a "Boss Attack List" to involve your boss in the prioritizing process.

3. Never say "Let me look into it" to a person who is trying to reverse delegate to you.

4. Concentrate on the 20% of your responsibilities that account for 80% of your value to your organization. It will keep your visibility and credibility high.

5. Use the 80/20 rule and the priority matrix to prioritize your activities.

6. Start using the "save-up" method to control "blurting" and encourage those around you to do the same.

7. Desperately fight your way back into Quadrants One and Two — the high-value quadrants.

4 THE DAILY PLAN
How to schedule your day

We're going to continue working our way toward making viable, realistic and effective daily plans. To get there, we need to consider three more important aspects of wise time management: prime time versus downtime, controllable time versus uncontrollable time, and a time log. These three concepts work together to help you make more out of every hour, every day. At the end of this chapter, I will suggest several tools to enhance your time management efforts. At this point, you may be thinking, "All these new tools and techniques are going to take more of my time than they'll save." Well, using them *does take time*. But I guarantee they will save more time than they take. In fact, with regular use, these tools will raise your time management consciousness to a higher level. The techniques will become automatic, and you'll save even more time in the long run. Let's begin.

Prime times and downtimes

Are you a "morning person" or a "night owl"? Do you finally wake up after that fourth cup of coffee? Do you have a nap attack every day before lunch, after lunch or late in the afternoon? We all seem to have those productive times and those not-so-productive times in our days. I like to call them prime times and downtimes. Each of us cycles through prime time and downtime throughout the day. For instance, even though you might "slump" just before lunch, you can probably look forward to another "prime time" later in the afternoon.

Prime times are those periods when you are at your best. You have a high energy level, you are alert and you feel good physically. You are usually the most productive during your prime times, assuming that your work environment during those times is conducive to productivity. If something about your work environment consistently saps your effectiveness during your prime times, you need to change your work environment to maximize your prime times. For example, you might need to find a place to avoid interruptions, a place where you can work diligently during your prime times.

How can you take maximum advantage of your prime times? Try to concentrate on tasks that are important, difficult or complex, or involve decision making.

What about downtimes? During your downtimes, you usually have low energy, you're not very alert, and you may feel a bit sluggish. You can still function and communicate during downtimes but you're just not at the top of your game.

Here's an example of downtime activity: You have several pages of data to enter into your computer. You can input this information without huge reserves of energy or enthusiasm. After all, you'll only need to read and type. Other downtime tasks include returning routine phone calls, opening or sorting mail (assuming you should be doing that at all), catching up on professional reading, filing documents and discussing "save-ups" with co-workers.

If you are a manager or supervisor, you are also responsible for seeing that your employees use their prime times and downtimes most effectively. Keep in mind that out of a group of 100 people, at least three-fourths of them will normally have an early morning prime time. In fact, for most people morning is one of the best prime times of the day. In spite of this, when do many bosses schedule routine weekly staff meetings? First thing in the morning. And they blow away what was probably a common prime time for several very expensive people. As a manager or supervisor, you need to find out when your people are most productive, and when they are in downtime mode. Then you can schedule tasks and activities to take advantage of their daily productivity rhythms.

For example, routine weekly staff meetings should be held when most of your people experience downtime. On the other hand, if you are meeting to conduct a 10- to 15-year strategic planning session, you might want to schedule that during a common prime time, since strategic planning is often important, difficult and complex. In short, knowing *what* to work on *when* is one of the best timesaving tools you have.

Do you have a midday prime time from about 11:00 am to 1:00 pm? If so, break for lunch out of sync with everybody else. That way you will get a double bonus: You'll have fewer interruptions with everyone else at lunch, and when you do decide to take a break, you won't have to fight the lunch-rush crowds. You will probably get three times as much of your Quadrant One and Two tasks accomplished during your prime time than at any other time. I'm not suggesting that you never go to lunch again with your co-workers, but when you have something difficult, urgent or complex to work on, take full advantage of your midday prime time.

Maybe you have a prime time at the end of the workday, between 3:00 and 6:00 pm. That's great, because it's also the period with the fewest interruptions. Again, most people have several prime times and several downtimes during the course of a day — and that's normal. (However, if your downtime is 8:00 am to 5:00 pm, you have another problem — and I'm probably not qualified to help you.)

Controllable versus uncontrollable time

Controllable time is what's left in your workday after subtracting all the time you spend responding to crises, dealing with interruptions and working on system-imposed activities like reports. Crises, interruptions and system-imposed tasks, then, account for uncontrollable time. Either you can't anticipate them or you can't avoid them — they are out of your control. In order to schedule your workload on a daily basis realistically, you need to know how much controllable time you have in an average workday. Over the course of a work week, some days you'll have more controllable time than others. What's important is the level at which things tend to balance out. That is your average controllable time. Keep in mind, controllable time is the only time actually available to you to accomplish to-do list tasks.

Many people are shocked to discover that only 15 to 25% of their workday is controllable time. Scheduling too many tasks or activities for the available controllable time leads to failure, frustration, discouragement, stress and guilt — and you don't need any of those. Being realistic about your limited controllable time will also help you concentrate on Quadrant One and Two activities, because clearly you will run out of controllable time before you run out of things to do.

To determine the average amount of controllable time in your workday, first assume that 50% of each day is controllable and 50% is not. Therefore, for an eight-hour workday, only four hours are available for to-do list activities. Assume that the remaining four hours will be absorbed by tasks outside your control. Make your daily plans accordingly. Then, analyze one work week and find out what percentage of your time is actually controllable — and make adjustments as necessary.

If you found during your test week that you were able to accomplish more than what you had planned, and were able to add on and accomplish additional tasks from your to-do list, then you clearly have more than 50% controllable time available to you. So next week, schedule for 60% controllable time and 40% uncontrollable time and see how that works. On the other hand, if you weren't able to complete what you had scheduled in the original 50% controllable time, then you'll need to make a downward adjustment. Over the course of four to six weeks, keep making adjustments until you are consistently able to complete what you've scheduled into your controllable time — no more, no less.

The time log

We've looked at prime time versus downtime, and also controllable time versus uncontrollable time. Now, take a look at the completed time log in Figure 6 (see page 48). The time log will take the information you've gained from the other two tools in this chapter and help you put it to work. Under the "Activities" heading, enter the tasks you perform on a daily basis. Leave the last activity space for "other." You can comment on the "other" activity in the "Notes/Priority Code" space.

Now go to the blank copy of the time log in Figure 7 (see page 49). In the left margin, next to the time increments, bracket those periods that fall within your prime times. Most prime times last from 45 to 90 minutes, depending on the individual.

Here's how to complete the time log. First, make copies of this blank time log (Figure 7) — enough to log three to five days. Record only one "X" for each 15-minute period, even if you worked on more than one activity during that period. Select the task that was most important or took the longest and put an "X" beneath that activity in the space provided.

Now go to the "Notes/Priority Code" column and enter the priority code (quadrant number) for that activity. Don't wait until noon or the end of the workday to record all your information at once. You will never remember what you did in each of those 15-minute increments.

The time log will give you a good indication of how you are using your time. As you analyze your data, look at what you worked on during any 15-minute increment. Notice its priority code. Are you working on high-priority tasks during prime times? Are you working to ensure that your prime times correspond as much as possible with controllable time? Executives and managers typically find that they work on the wrong kinds of activities during their prime times more than 50% of the time. That's a strong indication that they need to restructure their workday to capitalize on their prime times more effectively.

Your daily plan

Figure 8 gives an example of a daily plan. As you can see, the daily plan is far more formal and organized than the to-do list we covered in Chapter 3. Before you can create an effective daily plan, you need to assign every item on your to-do list a priority code (quadrant number). Action items that make their way onto your daily plan should all have Quadrant One and Two priority.

Next, assign each task a pure time estimate. In other words, estimate how long the task will take *without* interruptions. Knowing that interruptions will inevitably occur, you can add the expected interruption time back into your daily plan. Your goal is to schedule as many tasks as possible, based on pure time estimates, into the controllable time slots throughout your day. By doing so, you'll be able to schedule your day realistically and alleviate a lot of unnecessary guilt. The pure time estimate comes from the third column of your to-do list. On the right-hand side of the daily plan you'll find a schedule column, where you schedule time for to-do tasks. I recommend that you use 10- or 15-minute increments, whatever works best for you. Don't try to become any more precise than that.

Figure 6

Time log

Activities

Time	Planning	Meeting	Reports	Coordinating	Budget	Writing	Counseling	Reading	Inspection	Dictation	Computer	Travel	Mail	Other	Notes/Priority code
7:00 – 7:15															
7:15 – 7:30															
7:30 – 7:45							X								1
7:45 – 8:00							X								3
8:00 – 8:15							X								3
8:15 – 8:30		X													1
8:30 – 8:45		X													3
8:45 – 9:00		X													3
9:00 – 9:15		X													3
9:15 – 9:30		X													3
9:30 – 9:45														X	4 Phone Calls
9:45 – 10:00														X	1 "
10:00 – 10:15			X												1
10:15 – 10:30			X												4
10:30 – 10:45			X												4
10:45 – 11:00														X	3 Phone Calls
11:00 – 11:15												X			3
11:15 – 11:30						X									1
11:30 – 11:45						X									1
11:45 – 12:00						X									3
12:00 – 12:15														X	1 Business Lunch
12:15 – 12:30														X	1 "
12:30 – 12:45														X	1 "
12:45 – 1:00														X	1 "
1:00 – 1:15														X	1 "
1:15 – 1:30														X	1 "
1:30 – 1:45				X											1
1:45 – 2:00				X											1
2:00 – 2:15	X														2
2:15 – 2:30	X														2
2:30 – 2:45	X														2
2:45 – 3:00	X														2
3:00 – 3:15								X							1
3:15 – 3:30				X											1
3:30 – 3:45			X												3
3:45 – 4:00			X												3
4:00 – 4:15						X									2
4:15 – 4:30						X									2
4:30 – 4:45						X									1
4:45 – 5:00						X									1

PRIME { 7:00 – 8:15

PRIME { 9:30 – 11:15

PRIME { 2:00 – 4:00

Figure 7 ——————————————————————————————————

Time log

Activities

Notes/Priority code

Time	
7:00 – 7:15	
7:15 – 7:30	
7:30 – 7:45	
7:45 – 8:00	
8:00 – 8:15	
8:15 – 8:30	
8:30 – 8:45	
8:45 – 9:00	
9:00 – 9:15	
9:15 – 9:30	
9:30 – 9:45	
9:45 – 10:00	
10:00 – 10:15	
10:15 – 10:30	
10:30 – 10:45	
10:45 – 11:00	
11:00 – 11:15	
11:15 – 11:30	
11:30 – 11:45	
11:45 – 12:00	
12:00 – 12:15	
12:15 – 12:30	
12:30 – 12:45	
12:45 – 1:00	
1:00 – 1:15	
1:15 – 1:30	
1:30 – 1:45	
1:45 – 2:00	
2:00 – 2:15	
2:15 – 2:30	
2:30 – 2:45	
2:45 – 3:00	
3:00 – 3:15	
3:15 – 3:30	
3:30 – 3:45	
3:45 – 4:00	
4:00 – 4:15	
4:15 – 4:30	
4:30 – 4:45	
4:45 – 5:00	

Figure 8

Daily Plan		
Items from to-do list	**Pure time estimate**	**Schedule**

If you like, you can now add interruption time back into your time estimates. You are better able to do that now because you know exactly when during the day you are going to work on each task, and you can more readily predict the amount of time you'll need to allocate for interruptions. For example, let's assume that during the first part of the morning you're going to work on a 60-minute pure time estimate task. During that part of your day, you anticipate having about 30 minutes of interruptions. So you know that you'll need to block out a total of 90 minutes for the task. If you were to schedule the same task near the end of the workday, you might expect only 15 minutes of interruptions and would block out 75 minutes on your schedule.

You can also build interruption time back in for those periods when you are working on system-imposed activities. Of course, scheduling for crises is impossible because you never know when they will occur. But remember, crisis time is already accounted for and is represented on your schedule by blank space. Don't make the mistake of scheduling every 15-minute increment. You'll need blanks in your schedule to deal with crises as they arise.

The tickler file

An alternative method for daily planning is a "tickler" or "suspense" file. (See Figure 9). You'll need a 3" x 5" card file box with three sets of tabs: one set for the months of the year (January–December), one set for dividing the current month into days (1–31), and a set of alphabetical tabs (A–Z). You'll also need plenty of blank 3" x 5" action cards. Rotate the month tabs in your file so when you open the box, the tab for the current month is always in front. Immediately behind the current month tab are the numbered tabs that allow you to divide the current month into daily slots. As each month passes, you'll bring the current month forward and refile the numbered tabs behind the current month.

The A–Z tabs are filed behind the tabs for the remaining months. This alphabetized section is your completed action file. When you complete a project or task, I recommend filing the related action card or cards in the completed action section alphabetically by task. You will need to weed out

Figure 9 ———————————————————————————————

The ticker file

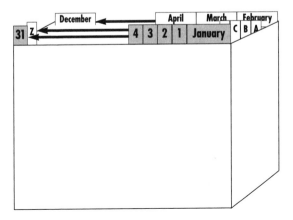

your completed action section periodically to keep those cards from overtaking the file.

That's how the tabs are set up, but how do action cards get into the file? Your boss may tell you today that she wants a project report from you by the end of the day a week from tomorrow. You don't even have to put that assignment on your to-do list. Create an action card that tells you what you have to do by when, and file it in the numbered section of the file on the date you need to start in order to finish the report on time. Give yourself an extra day to account for unexpected complications. If you create action cards for tasks you won't be starting in the current month, simply file them in the section tabbed by the relevant month and worry about exact-date filing during that month.

Other action cards will flow from your to-do list. When you are sure that you will have to complete an item from your to-do list and you have a specific deadline, create an action card for the task, file it in the appropriate place in your tickler box, and cross the task off your to-do list. Your tickler file will now track the task until it is completed. If the project will require multiple tasks with multiple deadlines, the action card, or set of cards for the project, will move from one deadline to the next until the project is complete. As you work on projects filed as action cards in your tickler file, you'll make progress notations on the action cards.

Note three things anytime you make a progress entry on an action card:

- Enter the current date.
- Record what you did to move the project along.
- Finally, make a note detailing what you'll need to do next, and by when.

If no further action is required for the particular task, refile the card in your completed action (A–Z) section.

Now that you have action cards in your tickler file, how do you use them to create daily plans for the next week? On

Thursday or Friday of this week, take out all your action cards for next week and separate them into five piles, representing the five days of the work week. To prioritize each day's action cards, lay them out on a flat surface and arrange the cards in the order you want to work on them. Keep priority codes and prime times in mind as you're arranging these cards.

In pencil on the face of each action card, enter the pure time estimate for that action. As you pick up the cards in order of their priority, keep a running total of the pure time estimates. *As soon as you've filled up the controllable time in your day, stop.* The stack is now your plan for that day. If any action cards are left over they must be reprioritized into action stacks for later in the week. Take care not to do carry-over actions first thing the next morning, because that means you have taken the lowest priorities from one day and automatically made them the highest priorities for the next day. *You must reprioritize.*

The tickler file combined with your daily plan is like a funnel. When you use them correctly, the tasks that are least urgent, least important and least likely to turn into a crisis fall out the bottom of the funnel. Remember what I told you earlier: You're not going to get everything done. With the tools I've given you in this chapter, you should have a clear focus on getting the *right* things done.

Actions to take now

1. Identify your prime times (for important, difficult, complex and urgent activities) and downtimes (for routine, system-imposed, "no-brainer" activities).

2. Determine the average amount of controllable and uncontrollable time you have in your workday.

3. Maintain a time log and fill it out in 15-minute increments for *three to five days*.

4. Make a daily plan for each day. Prioritize each task and give it a pure time estimate and time schedule.

5 ORGANIZING YOUR OFFICE AND DESK
How to reduce interruptions and gain control of your day

As you've probably gathered by now, taking control of your workday is not easy — but it can be done. In this chapter, we'll look at techniques you can use to reduce and control interruptions. We'll examine effective ways to deal with people who interrupt you, and finally, we'll look at proven techniques for sorting and attacking your paperwork.

Control interruptions by controlling your work space

The physical layout of your office

If you're a people-oriented individual, you have a natural, human tendency to set up your work space so that you face others in your work area, or face toward their pathways in your immediate area. You do that because you like people and it's uncomfortable to turn your back to them as they walk by your desk or office door. But that's exactly what you must do to be more productive.

Look at the physical arrangement of your work area. Is your desk positioned so that you are facing traffic? If it is, you'll be interrupted more often than if you were facing away. And when those interruptions occur, they drastically reduce the controllable work time in your day. Remember, it's not only the interruption time you lose, but also the recovery time to get back on track. When your desk faces traffic patterns, you are not only inviting interruptions, you're encouraging particularly slow-moving colleagues to waste tremendous amounts of your time. Why particularly slow moving? Because of what I call the "stir mode." Here's how it works: People who don't need to see you walk past your office to the break area to get coffee with cream or sugar, and go immediately into the stir mode. They slowly walk back down the hall, carefully stirring their coffee. Their pace is so slow that they can glance into absolutely every area along their path, whether it is an office or an open work area. When people are in stir mode, they not only move slowly, they think slowly. They are enjoying a break. Stirring coffee and being productive are mutually exclusive. Try it sometime.

Let's assume you are working at your desk, which faces your office door. Your head is down and you're working away. You hear a bit of commotion at your doorway. You finally look up. A person is already leaning against your door frame, still stirring. Two very powerful things happen next: First, you make direct eye contact with the other person. And eye contact is one of the most engaging aspects of body language. Second, and almost simultaneously, you exchange smiles or grins.

Together, eye contact and smiling constitute an invitation. Your co-worker is *still* stirring. Then "the question" flies. You've heard it a thousand times: "So, how's it going?" In the back of your mind you're thinking, "Oh boy, he's headed toward that comfortable chair." And if he sits down in your comfortable chair with that hot cup of coffee, when is he going to leave? About a week from Tuesday if you're lucky.

Have you experienced this scenario? Have you had people in "stir mode" sit down, get comfy and stay way too long? Is it more than just a little difficult getting them to leave without offending them? Here are a few techniques that will help.

Face away from traffic

Number one, the only reason you got that interruption in the first place was because you made eye contact. So, if you want to reduce unnecessary interruptions, the first thing you must do is minimize the opportunity for eye contact. Rearranging your office to face away from traffic will cut down on interruptions. Assuming your work space and furniture allow it, turn your desk around and put your back to traffic. If you can't bring yourself to do that, at least turn your desk sideways and put the traffic pattern off to the side in your peripheral vision. That too will help reduce the number of unnecessary interruptions you would otherwise have to deal with. The key here is: Don't make eye contact with people unless you really need to talk to them or they really need to talk to you.

Are your seats too soft?

I have a very good friend and client who I'll refer to as Amiable John. He is one of the most charming people I know. His staff dearly loves him. He's delightful. And he possesses all those wonderful people-oriented traits that tend to make him far less productive than he might be otherwise.

His staff likes to be around him so much that he found himself having far too many drop-in visitors who stayed far too long. His productivity was consistently driven down to almost zero. So John made a decision. Because he was so amiable and did not like to offend people, he hit on a creative — and subtle way — to let his people know they were overstaying their welcomes. John went to his grandmother's house and picked up an old hardwood, straight-backed kitchen chair. He brought the chair into his office and placed it diagonally off to the right of his desk. With a saw, he cut an inch and a half off the front legs. Can you picture his people sitting on that uneven chair, sliding down as they were talking to him? Sitting in John's uncomfortable, uneven chair isn't exactly conducive to shooting the breeze. John's unorthodox chair keeps visits short and visitors short-winded — all with tongue-in-cheek humor that his people appreciate.

John fully intended to use the chair only as long as it took for his staff to get the picture. Three and a half years later, the chair is still there, and his people still get a laugh out of it. More important, we had a chance to document John's interruption time and meeting time for three months before and after he brought the chair in. The result? John saved three weeks over the course of a year, all thanks to an uncomfortable chair.

Incidentally, when John did his "I wish I had" visualization exercise, one of the "I wish I hads" John wanted to prevent was, "I wish I had spent more time with my wife." Guess who got all three weeks worth of the time John saved? Mrs. Amiable John, of course. Here's the point: Time is there. Be creative and determined to go out and reclaim it.

Out of sight, out of *bind*

Here's another example of how to use physical layout to manipulate your work space to help control interruptions. I know a woman in Boston who runs her own company. She has a four-drawer filing cabinet placed just inside her office door. On the other side of the filing cabinet she keeps a nicely cushioned folding chair with arms. Aside from her own desk chair, the folding chair is the only place to sit in her office. When someone comes in to see her, she immediately rises. They start talking about whatever matters the visitor has to discuss, and then she makes a quick decision. If she wants to continue the conversation, she gets the folding chair, brings it out and offers the visitor a seat. If she wants to keep the conversation short, they both remain standing. This keeps most interruptions short, and she gets back to work faster.

Who's in control? She is. And control is the key factor when dealing with interruptions.

Who's lurking in your doorway?

What should you do when someone approaches you while you're talking on the phone and hovers over you while you are trying to carry on a phone conversation? The "Hoverer" shifts her weight from foot to foot, shuffles through papers and does just about anything to look busy. But she doesn't leave. If you have ever experienced a Hoverer, you already know that they are neither polite nor professional. What's the best way to handle this person? First, interrupt your phone conversation: "John, excuse me just a moment." Second, put your hand over the receiver and say, "Sheila, I'll be tied up with this call for a few minutes. Get back to me between 3 and 4 this afternoon and I'll be happy to listen." Third, break eye contact and return to your phone conversation, "Yes, John, what was that?" You have to break eye contact with "Hoverers," or they're going to continue lurking. You need to interrupt and let them know you are going to be on the phone for a while. But you'll be happy to help them during a time of day when you're more available to others.

A watched clock always foils

Do you have a clock in your work area? If you do, use it to shorten unwanted visits. Here's how: Place the clock on the wall opposite from where your visitors sit. Every once in a while during a conversation you want to end, you can turn and glance at the clock. Don't stare at it. And beware: We normally glance at clocks at exactly the wrong time and end up offending others. The guideline to follow, if you are going to avoid making enemies, is never to look at a clock while the other person is speaking. You can always glance at a clock while you are speaking and the other person won't feel uncomfortable. But your visitor will clearly sense your urgency. If you don't have a clock, you can do the same thing with a wristwatch.

Taming paperwork

Do people seem to crank out paperwork faster than you can read it or deal with it? During one of my seminars in Florida, a man named Bill shared his paper-taming system with me, and now I'll pass it on to you. It's a stroke of brilliance. Look at Figure 10. As you can see, Bill adapted the priority matrix from Chapter 3 to organize his paperwork. Imagine your desktop is divided into the same four quadrants as the priority matrix. Or, stack and number four separate in-boxes on your credenza. Whether you use piles at the tip of your desk or in-boxes behind you, the idea is to create four holding-places for paperwork.

Figure 10 ─────────────────────────────

Your desk

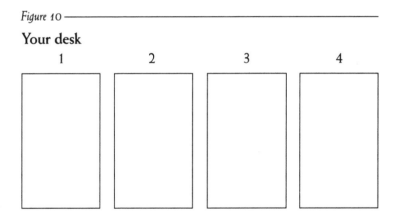

| 1 | 2 | 3 | 4 |

When paperwork shows up on your desk, scan it to determine its priority code, then put it into the appropriate quadrant pile at the top of your desk. First attack Quadrant One. If you finish what's there, and it's not time to deal with Quadrant Two paperwork (those are mid- and long-term items), move on to Quadrant Three. Bill almost never makes it to Quadrant Four — and you probably won't either — but that's okay. Remember, by definition, Quadrant Four paperwork is going to be both unimportant and not urgent. I told Bill, "That's a great system." He said, "Wait a minute, let me explain the system's real beauty. The most important part is that it gets rid of guilt." Bill related that when he used to get ready to leave his office in the evening, especially on Fridays, he would look at his desk and see a huge, seemingly all-important stack of paperwork. He would feel so guilty that he would go back to his desk, grab a big pile of paperwork, and jam it into his briefcase. He would reluctantly take it home and work on it over the weekend. Or worse, he'd find himself going back to the office over the weekend to attack that last big stack. Ever done the same things?

Now, at day's end, he reaches for that light switch, looks back at his desk, and gets immediate confirmation that he has remained focused on priorities all week long. You see, the Quadrant One stack is usually clear, and if it's not, he's waiting for something from someone else. If it's not Quadrant Two time, the paperwork in the Quadrant Two stack should be there. No reason to feel guilty about that. Quadrant Three is typically clear or almost clear. The Quadrant Four stack of papers is usually there, but who cares? Remember — never, ever work overtime on Quadrant Three or Four tasks.

Modern technology: friend or enemy?

Electronic communication has revolutionized the way we do business. But we need to control modern tools like e-mail, voice mail and faxing before they control us. In days gone by, passing documents back and forth through the mail would take three to five days in each direction. Today, we can fire correspondence back and forth as fast as we can type. That's pressure. Pressure to work faster. Pressure to respond. We begin to assume that just because something arrived electronically, it is more urgent and important than it might actually be. That's a mistake. A review of the average fax or e-mail message proves that we are able to communicate trivia at electronic speeds. You can't assume your Quadrant One paperwork will be filled with faxes, while the Quadrant Four pile is all conventional mail.

Furthermore, if not properly controlled, conveniences like e-mail, voice mail, pagers, fax machines and air-phones on commercial flights can end up being nothing more than "blurting" devices operating at blinding speeds. Technology meant to save you time will end up sabotaging you. The very tools meant to convey importance and urgency become meaningless.

I often wonder why anyone would transmit anything by e-mail unless it was both important and urgent — a Quadrant One issue. I wonder why people don't routinely identify the importance and urgency of the voice-mail messages they leave for others. And pagers should be used for emergencies only. At the very least, people should save up routine "beeps" and then page the person they want to reach once or twice a day with all the messages they want to deliver. Similarly, I wonder why an executive or manager would place a nonemergency call to the office from an air-phone when the call, in effect, expresses a lack of trust and confidence in the employees back at the office. My point is, we need to be certain that we are controlling these modern devices and using them to an advantage — not to interfere.

Laptop and notebook computers have given people on-line power outside the office. When you add portable dictation machines and cellular telephones, you can carry a well-equipped office right in your briefcase. With that in mind, I have a final word of caution regarding these extraordinary communication tools: If we use them together to work efficiently on high-priority tasks, they're terrific. But if we use them to work on low-priority activities that are quick, easy, interesting or merely entertaining, while placing high-priority tasks in jeopardy, then the tools have become little more than executive toys.

Action steps to take now

1. Rearrange your work area so you'll face away from traffic.

2. Get rid of comfortable chairs for visitors.

3. Stand when visitors enter, and remain standing to keep visits short.

4. Position your clock on the wall opposite where visitors sit. (But never look at a clock while the other person is talking.)

5. Organize your paperwork into four stacks, one for each priority quadrant.

6 MAINTAINING CONTROL
How to limit interruptions

In all likelihood, the people you work with are your most valuable assets. But when it comes to time management, they can also be a tremendous liability — the source of endless interruptions and unproductive visits. Since you will never be able to eliminate all interruptions (nor would you want to — many of them have tremendous value), the key to better time management lies in learning how to reduce interruptions, both in frequency and duration. In Chapter 5, I passed along ideas for arranging the physical layout of your work area to control interruptions. In this chapter you'll learn additional techniques for controlling both in-person and telephone interruptions to minimize the time you spend dealing with them. You'll also learn ways to make your phone calls shorter and more efficient. Plus, I'll share an innovative technique for "hiding out" from phone calls completely.

Close your door ... at least halfway

Do you have an office with a door you can close if you want to? Have you ever closed it to get some privacy — some quiet time — and afterwards felt guilty that you had shut everyone out? Here's a way to get rid of the guilt. Start by simply closing your door for a couple of days. Then, for the next couple of days, open the door just a bit. A couple of days after that, open the door a little more. Keep opening your door a little wider each day until you get it to a half-open position. Most people who start to interrupt will stop and treat that door as closed even though it's halfway open. And you'll feel great because you know it's open. No more guilt. What you have done is to mentally condition would-be visitors to know that the half-open door is as good as closed.

Using signals to control interruptions

What do you do if you don't have a door to close … even halfway? How do you control interruptions then? Signals are a great way to keep interruptions to a minimum. If you're going to use them, however, make sure everyone *knows* them. In other words, make sure everyone knows exactly what your signals mean, so they can play by the rules. Here's an example.

Remember my friend Amiable John? The first time John complained about interruptions eating up his time, I asked him, "John, would you be willing to close the door to your office?" He said, "No, I'm trying to maintain an open-door policy, and I would prefer not to close the door." So I said, "John, you don't have a secretary. If you don't want to close your office door, could you get a secretary who would physically screen people who are trying to interrupt you?" He said, "I probably could, but I would only need her services about half the day, so I couldn't justify the cost to my company."

I said, "So John, the only option you have is using signals. You need to determine what your signal is going to be, and you need to tell all your staff members what your signal is and what it means."

John came up with this signal: Whenever he is working in his prime, controllable time on something truly important, he simply puts on his baseball cap. When his employees see John with his hat on, they know he doesn't want to be interrupted. The hat is a simple but very clear signal.

Another friend of mine, who is the head of an administrative office, has a little flagpole on her desk. When the flag's up you can come in. When the flag's down you can't. I worked with a government agency in Washington, D.C. that used an extremely effective technique. The group works in a totally open office environment — no cubicles, no partitions, nothing but a large room full of desks. Each person in that room has a desk nameplate. If I walk up to Carol's desk, for example, and her nameplate is right side up, that means she's in her downtime and I can interrupt her (possibly to discuss save-ups). But if her nameplate is turned upside down, that means she is working on something very important and doesn't want to be interrupted unless it's an emergency.

When you use a signal to help control interruptions, do 100% of the people you work with respect that signal? No. But to whatever degree people do respect those signals on a daily basis, the time savings can be multiplied by 240-plus workdays a year. Even the smallest improvement in daily productivity adds up quickly.

Here's another creative and innovative signal to prevent interruptions. I learned this one from the employees in another federal agency. Their office space was arranged in four-person cubicles — a team-oriented arrangement. They bought small, styrofoam balls, spray-painted half the balls green and half of them red, and glued small magnets on the bottom. Each employee got a green ball and a red ball. Placing a red ball on top of the cubicle signaled, "no interruptions." A green ball on top of the cubicle signaled, "I'm in downtime. It's okay to interrupt me with save-ups." These government employees quickly learned that you have to play the game fairly. You can't put the red ball up and leave it there 100% of the time. Why? Because nobody will respect the signal. More than 65% of the time, the employees in that office respect the signal. At that rate, they calculated that they increased productivity about an hour-and-a-half to two hours a day per employee, all from a simple, inexpensive signaling system. When a fellow employee forgets about respecting the signal, all it takes is a gentle reminder: "I know you didn't mean to interrupt, but please notice that the red ball is up. I really would appreciate it if you would respect that signal, and I will do the same for you." It's not aggressive; it's politely assertive to teach the other person how you want to be treated.

Go visit them

Another simple tip for gaining control of your time is to visit others in their work area instead of in yours. Assume that somebody calls you and says, "Can I come by to see you?" Instead of your usual, "Sure, come on down," try saying, "Hold on, I was just headed your way. I'll be there in about two minutes." When you are the visitor, you are in control. It's a lot easier to leave someone else's office than it is to get them out of the comfortable chair in *your* office.

So how do you respond to that dreaded question, "Got a minute?" There are several proven possibilities. You could just say "No," but that's a bit blunt. Nevertheless, you might need to be blunt with the person who has been a persistent pest. When the answer is clearly no, a good way to respond is with what I call the "no plus an option" response: "No, I can't see you at the moment, however, I could see you at ..." Then you'd suggest a couple of time slots during your downtime. It's important for you to memorize your downtimes so you don't accidentally give away your prime times. It's nice to offer the person two options and let him or her make the choice. It makes people feel better about your initial refusal to listen.

When you are dealing with people who always seem to come to you with Quadrant Three or Four matters, or try to get you to do their work, use the same technique but offer them a time to get back with you that's close to their quitting time. "No, I can't see you now, but I could see you at five o'clock, if you could come back then." Most likely, they won't take the time to come back and see you at quitting time. Only those people who want to discuss Quadrant One and Two issues will. And more often than not, you'll find that those people with Quadrant Three and Four problems will solve them overnight. Or they'll decide that the issue wasn't that important to begin with.

In my view, assuming you're at a point in your day where an interruption is okay, the best response to "Got a minute?" is, "I have just a couple of minutes, how can I help you?" Rather than giving them a precise amount of time, "just a couple of minutes" helps you maintain control. In other words, you can dictate exactly how long a "couple of minutes" will be. If you can only squeeze in a quick visit, you've already set the stage for that. If you have time for a longer interruption, you can let "a couple of minutes" become 20 minutes if you so choose. The point is, you're in control.

How to end visits in your office

The discussion is closed

You cannot, of course, totally eliminate visits to your office or work area. But there are still more ways for you to gain some measure of control over their duration. For example, if someone wants to visit you regarding some paperwork, place the papers in a manila folder prior to the meeting and leave the file open on your desk during the discussion. When you're ready to wrap up the conversation, briefly summarize key points while you close the file to a vertical position in front of you. Closing the file makes a strong impression. Your visitor will have no doubt that the discussion — like the file folder — is closed.

Stroll them out of your office

What about people who still don't get the message? The people who won't leave, no matter how many files you close? It happens to everyone. And when it does, it's time to use the four-step strolling routine. You can use these four steps not only for lagging visitors, but also with people who keep you on the telephone too long.

Step 1: Stand up

Let's assume a person is sitting in your office, and the conversation is getting repetitive. You want it to end quickly. The first thing you should do is stand up. Standing, if nothing else, will change the status quo. Something is about to happen, even if your visitor's not quite sure what.

Step 2: Stroll and summarize

After standing up, immediately begin a slow stroll, an amble. Slow pace is important — you don't want to do anything rude or abrupt. By this time, your visitor will be standing alongside you. It's pretty difficult to stay seated while someone else is standing and walking away. Now it's time to summarize. When I say summarize, I don't mean you need to recap the entire conversation. You only need to mention a point or two to control the conversation until you have the visitor up and walking with you. An example might be, "Phyllis, the point you made about needing improved inventory control was an excellent one." If you are in a small work space, you can even start the summary while you begin to stand up in Step 1.

Step 3: Stroll and compliment

Continue the stroll and move toward your work area exit. Your strolling won't stop until you and your visitor have left your work area. To control the conversation in Step 3, compliment your guest. For example, "Phyllis, that report you sent me Wednesday helped me to meet my boss's deadline on an important project. You did a great job." Complimenting your guest will give you control of the conversation until you reach the exit from your work area.

Step 4: Thank them

When you get your visitor out of your work space, thank them. Short and sweet is fine: "Phyllis, thanks for coming by. I'll talk to you later." Or if you want to take pains to smooth any potential ruffled feathers: "Phyllis, thanks so much for stopping by. It's always nice to chat with you. I hope you'll forgive me for running along. I'm a bit behind schedule today. But thanks for coming by. Take care." Whether your thanks are brief or elaborate, the next critically important step is to break eye contact, turn and go. If you linger, the visitor is likely to try to continue the conversation.

Despite all these carefully crafted techniques, you'll sometimes have visitors who simply won't budge. They're as immovable as the Rock of Gibraltar. Here's what happens with the Rock: You wrap up the conversation, go through the four-step stroll-them-out technique and get the Rock out of your work area. You're halfway back down the hall, you turn around, and guess what? The Rock is still there. What could you possibly have done wrong? You have been sending all kinds of verbal and nonverbal signals to let this person know the conversation is ending — including strolling out of your work area and saying goodbye — and the Rock hasn't picked up the first clue. When hints and gestures fail, you must be insistent: "Peter, I really do hate to insist, but there is another very important matter I need to work on. I'm sure you'll understand. We'll talk again soon. Thanks for coming by." Notice I said *another* important matter. The word *another* is important because it tells Peter that he too is important. Just because we sometimes have to be assertive doesn't mean we have to insult people. So be sure to insert the word *another*. Now, break eye contact, turn and go.

How to control telephone interruptions

Most of the techniques you use for ending meetings in your office also work on the telephone. You can even use the four-step stroll routine with people on the telephone to terminate a long-winded conversation. Of course, you won't literally stroll callers off the phone, but you should, however, stand up when you want to end a phone conversation. Why? To make sure you're not the one making the conversation longer than it needs to be.

Tape record your phone conversations for a day

I remember complaining to a friend one time about people who kept me on the telephone too long. People were always asking more questions, always extending the conversation, always making extra comments. My friend said, "Are you sure it's those other people? Or is it you?" To find out who was guilty of lengthening my phone conversations, he suggested I place a small tape recorder on my desk and record my side of all telephone conversations for one day. *Warning: It's illegal to tape a caller's voice unless you get prior approval, so only record your side of the conversation.* I took his suggestion and made a shocking discovery. When the conversation was dying down, I heard myself continuing to ask questions and extending our discussion. My callers weren't the problem at all. I was. Are you the problem too? Find out for yourself.

Hiding out

One of my consulting clients uses an innovative concept they call Available Work Surfaces. At this company, many employees travel extensively. At any given time, several desks, cubicles and offices are left empty. These empty work spaces are terrific places to hide — quiet places where individuals know they will have controllable, uninterrupted time. Here's how the Available Work Surfaces concept works: When people travel and will be gone for more than 24 hours, they must clear their desks. Everything goes in the desk and the desk is locked. That desk then becomes a numbered, available work surface. If another employee is working on something important and needs quiet, uninterrupted time, the person simply calls the receptionist and asks where to work. The receptionist assigns one of the available work surfaces — and the beautiful thing is that employees don't have to tell anyone where they're going. They make themselves unreachable. The company estimates that the Available Work Surfaces concept has improved productivity by about two hours a day per person.

Train your telephone screeners

The most important way to gain control over telephone interruptions is to train your telephone screeners. As an independent management consultant, I once spent four-and-a-half years calling literally thousands of businesses and organizations. I found that most telephone screeners have received little or no training. First, they would usually answer the phone incorrectly. Second, they would ask the wrong questions.

How to answer the phone

Let's assume I make a phone call and say, "Good afternoon, this is Dick Lohr. I'm calling from the ABC Company. May I please speak with Bob Phillips?" If the secretary is trying to screen the call, she will usually ask, "Mr. Lohr, what is this in reference to?" Or, "What's the nature of your call?" I could spend 10 minutes explaining the nature of my call, but the screener still would have no idea whether or not to put my call through.

What truly matters is the priority of my call. An effective telephone screener needs information to help gauge where the call would fit in the boss's priority matrix (which quadrant). If it's a Quadrant One matter, the call should go through. If it's a Quadrant Two, Three, or Four matter, the screener should take a message so Bob can call me back at his convenience, during one of his downtimes.

So how does the screener determine priority? Should the

screener say, "Mr. Lohr, is this important?" No. Because I would say, "Well, would I have called if it weren't important?" Most of us consider the subjects of our phone calls important, no matter how unimportant our calls may be to the people we are calling. So, screeners should never question the importance of incoming calls. They can, however, prioritize a phone call in terms of its urgency.

The screener might say, "I'm sorry, Mr. Lohr, Bob is unavailable at the moment. Do you need a response to this matter within the next hour?" Asking this pointed question helps define urgency — and helps keep people honest. Though you will always have callers who inflate the urgency of their calls, most will respond, "Well, it's not really all that urgent. Tell you what, it's just important that I talk to Bob today."

"Fine, Mr. Lohr, I know Bob will be making his return calls between 3:00 and 5:00. Do you expect to be at your phone then?" By setting up a bracketed time for the return call, Bob and I don't get involved in an endless cycle of telephone tag.

Now, what if I respond to the telephone screener with, "Yes, I need to resolve this matter within the hour" or "Yes, it's an emergency." The screener now knows exactly what priority my call is: It's urgent and important. The screener would put the call through directly or have the call returned within an hour as promised. Bingo. It's done. Never underestimate the importance of training your telephone staff to help you manage time wisely.

Set preferred calling times

Whenever possible, tell people the best times to reach you (always during your downtimes). You can say something like, "Mary, I know it's sometimes difficult to get through to me. Let me give you some times when it's easier to get hold of me." Then pass on several downtimes. And one of the ways to make sure you get most of your calls during downtimes is to make it difficult for people to get through to you during your prime times. But be consistent. If I convince you to call during my downtimes and you call me during my prime time — and I let you get through with no problem — what's the message? Call anytime.

Group your outgoing calls

Grouping outgoing calls is a good way to save time, and you can also save time by doing similar or identical activities within a compressed period of time. Examples include writing letters, preparing memos, completing reports, etc. You get into a "groove" and improve your efficiency. If you spread similar or identical activities over the entire workday, you lose this efficiency.

You can even get a bonus in time savings if you group outgoing calls near the end of the workday — and especially during the last hour on Friday. Even the most people-oriented and chatty conversationalists look forward to the weekend. No one is likely to waste time on the phone at 4:30 on Friday. As a result, you can take care of a large number of calls during the last hour on Friday.

Telephone socializing

As I mentioned in Chapter 3, depending on your purpose, socializing can be a Quadrant Four waste of time, or a truly important and urgent, Quadrant One activity. The same holds true on the phone. One of the best ways to control your telephone social life is simple: Stand up during the telephone call. Marilynn, a college professor, once told me, "You know, Dick, from the very first day I got into the academic world, I realized that if I would simply stand up for my telephone calls, I could save tremendous amounts of time every year. I also realized," she said, "that I didn't have enough self-discipline or willpower to make myself stand up. So, I was spending far too much time on the phone."

What she lacked in self-discipline and willpower, however, she made up for in creativity. Marilynn went to the university carpenters and had them build a pedestal by the side of her desk. They mounted the telephone on top of the pedestal, which was so high she could not reach the telephone to answer it or dial it from a sitting position. The last time I saw Marilynn I asked her, "Marilynn, how much time do you think you got out of that pedestal per year?" She said, "About 10 days." She confirmed something I've always suspected — maximizing your time calls for maximum creativity.

Plant seeds to finish telephone calls

Bringing a telephone conversation to an end can sometimes be difficult. But there are ways to plant seeds that signal you're about to finish the conversation. Here are two of my favorites: 1) "Carol, before we hang up ..." The first seed is planted. Or you might say, "Before we hang up, there was one additional item I wanted to quickly mention to you." It works like a charm. 2) Another technique that is especially respectful of the other person goes like this: When a conversation has gone on a little too long and has become repetitive, say, "I know you're busy, I'll let you run." You're acknowledging the value of the other person's time and saving your own time, too.

Actions to take now

1. Be assertive and learn to say no.

2. Use a signal system to let people know when you don't want to be interrupted.

3. Visit others in their work areas instead of in yours.

4. Close your door, at least halfway.

5. Use the four-step stroll-them-out-of-your-office process.

6. Tape record *your* side of phone conversations for one

day to see if you are making conversations longer than necessary.

7. Use the Available Work Surfaces concept to escape interruptions.

8. Train your telephone screeners how to determine a call's priority code.

9. Ask people to call you during your downtimes.

10. Group outgoing calls at the end of the day when others won't be tempted to linger.

11. Plant seeds to finish telephone conversations.

7 DELEGATION
How to gain time with the help of your team

In the previous chapter, I suggested you train your telephone screeners to help you manage time more effectively. There's a significant lesson in this, one more important than simply managing telephone calls. The lesson is this: Sometimes we need to let others help us manage our time wisely. We actually need to give up a measure of control to gain more control in the long run. For most of us, this can be a frightening — and initially time-consuming — process. But I guarantee you, soliciting help — delegating — is one of the best things you can do to make the most of your time at work and at home.

About half of the battle in delegating effectively is knowing how to do it. The other half is developing the mind-set to make it happen. Do you believe that most good ideas come from the top and not from the bottom or front line of the organization? Do you believe that the organization will be successful only if the employees do what management tells them? Do you believe that, by delegating, management gives up both power and control? If you answered yes to any of these questions, you'll have a hard time delegating effectively. If your mind-set is just the opposite, then delegation will come easily. For delegation to work, you must believe it is, in fact, a way to liberate the talents and abilities of your people, and learn just how remarkable they can be. With that in mind, let's focus on the delegation process.

Use three major steps to delegate effectively:

Step 1: Give up responsibility

Let me be very clear about the meaning of giving people responsibility. Giving responsibility is not a matter of picking up a stack of paperwork, throwing it out the door and saying, "Somebody handle this." That's called dumping, not delegating. Dumping says, "Here are more Quadrant Three and Four issues for you to handle."

Now, I'm not saying you can't delegate low-priority, low-urgency tasks. I'm simply suggesting that you delegate them to people who will be challenged and excited by them. What's become boring and simple for you might be interesting and complex for someone else. When you delegate a project, make sure you convey enthusiasm and a sense of respect. Avoid, even unconsciously, making a delegate feel like they're stuck with all the make-work you simply don't want to do. Delegates need to feel important and involved. They need to know the job you've given them contributes to the organization's success.

Every so often, verify that you are delegating meaningful, significant and important work to your employees — even Quadrant One and Two tasks and projects. Most of us think we already do that. But this is one area where the reality can be significantly different from the perception. So, as I've suggested with other concepts, set up a way to monitor what you're delegating. Periodically, maintain a 30-day delegation log. Create a separate delegation log for each of your employees, put them all in a folder and keep it on your desk. Each time you delegate, go to the appropriate employee's log and enter what you delegated, along with its priority code. At the end of the month, simply go back and add up the number of Quadrant One (or parts of Quadrant One) tasks you delegated. Then look at how many Quadrant Two, Three and Four tasks you delegated. If you're typical, you'll probably find that you delegated mainly Threes and Fours. Should you have delegated the Threes and Fours? Yes. But you need to delegate Quadrant One or Two tasks too, if your employees are ever to develop and grow professionally.

If you find you are not delegating enough Quadrant One and Two tasks, the solution is easy. Go back to your time log and scan the right-hand column for Quadrant One and Two tasks. Decide which ones you could delegate — in whole or in part — to your employees. You may realize that your people need additional training in some areas before you increase the responsibilities you are sharing with them. Fine. Train them. The time you spend will be time you save in the long run.

Step 2: Give up authority

Whenever you give an employee responsibility, you should also give the employee something else: authority. Authority is important because when you give both responsibility and authority, you can hold your employee accountable. Have you ever worked for a boss who delegated a project to you, told you what to do, when to do it, where to do it, why you must do it and how to do it? In effect, your boss put you in a tiny box, then had the audacity to tell you to be creative. You can't be creative in a tiny box or when you have no authority. You can't do a job the way you think it should be done. Delegating without giving authority makes people puppets. That's neither smart nor fair.

Insecure, power-hungry leaders are particularly susceptible to delegating without also giving up authority. In this situation, the delegate is automatically in a no-win situation. No matter what your leadership style is, double-check yourself when you're delegating and make sure you're also giving authority when you assign responsibilities.

Step 3: Demand accountability

Power-hungry delegators have no difficulty with this third step. They are very good at holding people accountable for results. Relationship-oriented leaders, on the other hand, do well in assigning responsibility and in granting authority, but usually have some difficulty with this third step. The reason? They have an intense need to be liked, and they hate any kind of confrontation. When they delegate a task and it's done incorrectly, rather than confront the delegatee, they redo the task themselves and say nothing to the delegatee. They let people off the hook. Do you fall into this trap? If so, I urge you to change. When you ignore accountability, you're helping no one. You're wasting your time — and you're allowing them to fail. Demanding accountability has to do with your perception of how best to help your people develop and grow. If you take that responsibility seriously, you'll be willing to hold your employees accountable for results, even at the risk of being disliked. The bottom line is that you need to be willing to risk not being liked, and that's a tough challenge for most of us.

Here's something to make it easier. For a few minutes, think about people in your life who were always easy on you. They didn't set any high standards for you — artistically, socially, academically, athletically — nor did they require you to set any high standards or expectations for yourself. Every time you tried something new and ran into a problem or unexpected challenge, everything inside of you was saying, "I want to quit. I don't want to do this any more. I want to throw in the towel."

At the same time, those "easy" people in your life were saying, "Go ahead, quit. No one else cares anyway. Two or three years from now, no one will know the difference." But most of the time you didn't quit. You forged ahead and you got the job done, despite people who were willing to let you off the hook. They were low-impact people. They had precious little to do with any success you have enjoyed in your life, personally or professionally.

The question I always ask myself about the low-impact people is, "Do I remember their names?" The answer almost always is no. Now let's turn the coin over. Think about people in your life who pushed you — and pushed you hard. They set high standards for you or made you set high standards for yourself. I'm not saying you *liked* them then — or that you ever will. But 10, 20 or 30 years from now, I'll bet you will remember their names. And second, I'll bet you respect them. Why? Because they were high-impact people in your life. They had a lot to do with the success you achieved.

I remember one of those high-impact people in my life. Her name was Helen. She taught me to play classical music on the piano. I remember when I was about 12, I was sitting at her grand piano, desperately trying to play what I thought was a difficult, complex and boring classical exercise. While I was playing, Helen put her hand on my forearm and said, "Let me interrupt you, Dick. I would like you to play the left hand softer than the right." Imagine that. I was a 12-year-old, clumsy, uncoordinated little boy. It was all I could do just to hit the keyboard and she wanted me to play the left hand softer than the right. In my view, I would never be able to do that, and at that point I made a very bad mistake. I said, "I can't."

Helen jumped out of her chair, assumed a domineering stance, put her hands on her hips and said, "Young man, don't you ever, ever tell me 'I can't.' I know you have the talent to play the left hand softer than the right, and you are going to go home right now and practice, practice, practice until you can play the left hand softer than the right. And when you come back here next week, I will sit right here and listen to you play the left hand softer than the right. Your lesson for today is over. Go home."

That week I did everything but sweat bullets learning to play the left hand softer than the right. I knew better than to walk back into her house without being able to play the left hand softer than the right. So, by the end of my week's practice, I could do it. But that's not the moral of the story. The point is that in my adult life, there were many times when I was confronted with challenges and all I wanted to do was quit — just throw in the towel. But I didn't. Not because I was strong — I wasn't. Rather, it was because I was lucky enough to have had someone like Helen in my life, standing there in the back of my mind saying, "Young man. Don't you tell me 'I can't.' "

I'm asking you to become a high-impact person in the lives of your employees, like Helen was in mine. To become that high-impact person, and to help your people become not just as good as they thought they could be, but far better than they ever dreamed they could be, you will have to risk being disliked. Your responsibility in this case is not only to yourself. It's to your people.

Completed staff work

Now, back to the delegation process itself. In Chapter 3, I discussed sources of to-do list items. One source was subordinate-imposed tasks. Your learned that some subordinate-imposed tasks are the result of work being thrown back into your lap — reverse delegation. The three questions you can use to prevent reverse delegation form a system I call completed staff work. You should memorize these questions, because you will have many opportunities to use them as you delegate.

I don't take credit for these three questions. They were apparently used frequently by Napoleon, who used them when communicating with his staff. When one of his people ran into a problem with a task Napoleon had assigned, he would ask them:

1. Give me a clear statement (description) of the problem.

2. What are the alternative solutions, and what are the advantages and disadvantages of each alternative?

3. What is your recommendation and why?

We don't live in Napoleonic France, of course. But completed staff work still works like a charm. Suppose Karen works for me. I have delegated a task to her that will take two weeks to complete. She starts on the project. On Thursday of the first week I'm ready to leave my office for a very important meeting. On my way out, Karen intercepts me halfway down the hall and says, "Dick, remember that two-week project you delegated to me?" "I sure do, Karen." She says, "Well, I ran into a problem with it. Let me tell you about it." "Okay," I say, "I've got to be in a very important meeting shortly, but go ahead."

Karen begins to explain what's going on. As she's talking, I realize that the problem is something she probably could have handled herself. Now I look at my watch and find that I'm late for my meeting. So I say to Karen, "I'm late for my meeting. Tell you what (here come the five killer words) let me look into it." Not only was Karen trying to reverse delegate the project to me, but in essence I raised my hand and volunteered to take it back with those five killer words.

What should I have done? I should have demanded completed staff work: "Karen, what's a clear statement of the problem?" She explains. "Karen, what alternatives do we have?" She says, "Well, boss, I think we could do A, we could do B, or we could do C." Great. "What are the advantages and disadvantages of those three alternatives?" She says, "I've been so busy that I haven't had a chance to look into them yet." Notice that I'm not going to say, "Let me look into them." Instead, I say, "Karen, why don't you go ahead and look into those advantages and disadvantages and also come up with your recommendation. Then, let's get together at 10:00 tomorrow morning to discuss it."

I made an appointment with Karen for 10 am because Karen was trying to delegate the project back up to me. If I hadn't made the appointment, which gave her a clear deadline for completing her staff work, Karen could have easily avoided doing what was necessary to solve the problem.

When we meet the next morning she'll have her recommendations and solutions. And I won't forget to compliment her because that's the kind of behavior I want to see more of. Old habits die hard of course, but the next time Karen thinks about reverse-delegating a project to me, she's going to remember that I'll insist on completed staff work. In time, Karen will answer all three questions right from the start. And that will give me another opportunity to compliment her.

When you consistently require completed staff work from your employees, you'll become a high-impact person in their lives. You'll teach them how to become part of a problem's solution rather than part of the problem. Completed staff work is also a wonderful antidote to people who like to criticize or tear things apart without giving any thought or effort to how they could improve things. Completed staff work keeps people focused on solutions.

By the way, remember to apply completed staff work to yourself, too. Before you go to see your boss with an issue, make sure you have a recommendation and avoid the temptation to merely voice your concerns, complaints or problems. Never approach your boss with issues until you have answered the three completed staff work questions. Your boss won't always support your recommendation, but he or she will never be able to accuse you of not doing your homework or not being prepared — an embarrassing proposition for any professional.

Actions to take now

1. Create a delegation log to make sure you're delegating challenging assignments — and enough of them.

2. Prevent reverse delegation by insisting on completed staff work.

   a. Explain the problem.

   b. What are the alternative solutions, and the advantages and disadvantages of each?

   c. What is your recommendation and why?

3. Before presenting a problem, issue or concern to your boss, be sure to answer the completed staff work questions yourself.

8 CONTROLLING MEETINGS
How to plan, conduct and end them

In Chapter 3, we learned how to control "blurting," one of today's greatest productivity drains. Now it's time to address the second great productivity leech: meetings. An effective meeting can produce a tremendous return on the time you and your staff invest. But all too often, just the opposite is true. Many meetings are just not worth your time.

Complaints about meetings

Think about what's wrong with the meetings you attend. Most people complain that meetings are too long. No hard and fast rules exist to determine the perfect length for meetings. I can only encourage you to get out of the Automatic Hour rut. More specifically, don't assume that every meeting needs to be an hour. Some will be shorter, and others will be longer — and still effective. Frankly, if you use the meeting planning tool I suggest later in this chapter, your meetings will naturally end at reasonable times because they'll stay better focused.

Another common complaint about meetings is that they never start on time. So, how do you start meetings punctually? Simple: Start them on time, then lock the door. If people haven't made prior arrangements to arrive late, they simply don't get in.

When people get locked out of meetings, two things happen. First, they are embarrassed. Even people who are habitually tardy rarely risk this sort of public embarrassment twice. Second, latecomers who are locked out of meetings will need to ask others for help later. After the meeting, the shamed offender has to go to one of his co-workers who attended the meeting and say, "I was late again today and I missed the meeting. Can you tell me what took place?" After a while, his peers are going to say, "No, I don't have time to go through the meeting twice. Why don't you show up on time?" With that kind of peer pressure, you can bet people will show up to meetings on time. Locking latecomers out of meetings is simple and effective — and chances are good you won't have to do it for very long.

Here's another tip: Begin your meetings at unusual times. Try 8:07 instead of 8:00 or 8:15. The message you will communicate is that the meeting is not going to start around 8:00, or a little after 8:00. It is going to start at precisely 8:07, so be there at or before that particular time. People take for granted that their watches are accurate enough to get them to a meeting right at 8:00. Yet, they aren't sure their watches are accurate enough to get them there at exactly 8:07. Most will show up a little early and the meeting can start on time.

Other complaints about meetings include: inviting the wrong people, inviting too many people, ending without clear-cut assignments, being derailed by hidden agendas, and so on. People also resent meeting attendees who are ill-prepared. Here are some tips to help you combat most of these complaints.

The meeting plan

A solid meeting plan will eliminate most, if not all, the complaints I just mentioned. Figure 11 (on page 88) shows an example of the Meeting Plan that I recommend. Let's go through each point:

Purpose

If you can't write down the specific purpose of the meeting, what should you do? Cancel the meeting. Take that weekly staff meeting every Tuesday morning at 9:15. You and your staff get together whether you need the meeting or not. People show up, there's no agenda (except for hidden ones), the content meanders, then everyone rushes back to their offices to try to catch up on the day's work. Next week, the process repeats itself. Do everyone a big favor — never hold a meeting without having a precisely stated purpose.

Participants (expected contribution)

Here, you simply list who is expected to attend and what each person is expected to contribute at the meeting. Remember the 80/20 rule from Chapter 3? Let's apply it to meetings. Eighty percent of a meeting's value is generated by only 20% of those at the meeting. If a person has only a small amount of input to offer during a meeting or will get only a small amount of output, why should the person sit through the entire meeting? You have several options.

Ask people to give written input. It takes less time to create half a page of notes than to attend an hour-long meeting. Or, one person can represent several other would-be participants. If it's still necessary for people with only a small amount of input to attend the meeting, let them speak at the beginning of the meeting, then release them back to work. If you do this, don't forget to make a note on the chairperson's meeting plan to excuse people after their presentations.

Here's my favorite way to get input from someone who doesn't need to attend the entire meeting — it also saves the most time and money: Put the input on a cassette tape. When meeting participants want to hear the input, they can play the tape at their convenience. If they have questions

Figure 11

Meeting Plan

Purpose:

Participants: (expected contribution)

Estimated cost: $

Desired outcome:

Agenda:

Date:
Time:
Location:

regarding the input, they can contact the appropriate individual following the meeting. And, as you will see below, there is another good reason to have a tape recorder at the meeting.

Estimated cost

I never used to include this item on the Meeting Plan. Then I went to work for an organization that ran some of the most unproductive meetings I'd ever experienced. I kept urging the boss to improve the situation. He agreed, but nothing ever seemed to change. One of my colleagues said, "Why don't you do something to get the boss's attention?" "Like what?" I asked. He replied, "Let him know how much the unproductive meetings actually cost. Bosses almost always pay attention to dollars and cents."

So I went to the Finance folks and asked if they could tell me how much each person who attended our meetings cost per minute, including salary and perks. Salary information was already in their database, so it was easy to make the calculations on a per-minute basis. Of course, they couldn't reveal individual salaries — that was confidential, and probably is at your organization, too. But they gave me per-minute averages for entry-level people, middle managers, executives and so forth. Thereafter, whenever a Meeting Plan came across my desk, I could determine the *group cost* per minute depending on who was invited to the meeting. Then all I had to do was multiply that cost by the number of minutes we planned to meet, and voilá, I had the meeting cost.

The first time I showed the group cost of a meeting to my boss, he nearly choked. The cost of 15 mid-level managers meeting for an hour and a half was $1,460. And that was some 25 years ago. Salaries have risen considerably since then. I doubt that in this day and age we could put 15 mid-level managers in a meeting for 90 minutes for less than $2,500. My boss almost came unglued. He grabbed his red pen and started deleting participants. He went to the agenda and started crossing off items. He said, "I can't afford this,

Dick." I said, "Sir, that's what I've been trying to tell you." Seeing meeting costs in cold, hard cash is sure to trim agenda items and cut down on the number of participants.

Desired outcome(s)

The Participants (expected contribution) section of the Meeting Plan describes the input expected from each person during the meeting. The Desired Outcome(s) section describes exactly what you hope to accomplish at your meeting. It might be something like "Decide which word processing software to install on the computer system," or "Eliminate $3,000 in overruns from the proposed department budget." Given the cost of the meeting, we need to decide if the expected output is worth the cost. If it's not, don't hold the meeting. Instead, find a less expensive way to generate the necessary decisions or actions.

Agenda

People often complain that meetings get off track. But when you ask, "Did you have an agenda?" The answer is often no. Well, if you didn't have an agenda, how did you know when people got off track? And how did you know when they got back on track? Every meeting needs to have a definite agenda.

The agenda details each matter you'll cover in a meeting. Once you set the agenda, you'll have a clear-cut idea of whom to invite. For people who might need to know about only a fraction of the agenda items, that tape recorder will come in handy again. Use one with a digital counter and be sure to start the counter at zero before the meeting begins. Assign one person to record (in writing) each agenda topic that surfaces during the meeting. As you move from item to item, log the counter number next to the topic listing. After the meeting, send the topic listing and the tape to those who need only a small amount of information from the meeting. They can fast-forward the tape to the topics they need to hear, then rewind the tape and send it on to the next person. An added benefit to recording meetings is that people will stick to business rather than chit-chat or socialize when they know they're on tape.

Do you need a Meeting Plan for emergency meetings? The answer is, "sorta." You need part of the Meeting Plan to prevent even emergency meetings from getting off track. Before calling an emergency session, take a couple of minutes to identify your purpose, the desired outcome and the meeting's supporting agenda. At the very least, complete those three sections on the Meeting Plan.

Date, time, location

Administrative details about your meeting are important. List not only the date, but the day of the week. List a start time and a stop time. And specify the exact location for the meeting. Make it as easy as possible for people to attend.

What to do before, during and after the meeting

Before the meeting

An effective meeting requires advance planning. Before the meeting (three to five days ahead), prepare and distribute the Meeting Plan. Distribute it earlier if the participants need extensive preparation time.

During the meeting

First, start on time. Second, stick to the agenda and the exact schedule for agenda items, if one has been assigned. Let's assume that Phyllis brings up a non-agenda item. You should listen briefly to what Phyllis says, then reply, "Phyllis, that's a very interesting point. Possibly we could include that in a future meeting agenda. However, today I'd like to return to agenda item number two which is ..." Notice that you didn't put her down. You didn't say Phyllis's point was unimportant.

You merely suggested that the topic be included in a future meeting agenda. Third, if you don't lock the door at the start of the meeting, then don't catch up latecomers. If you stop the meeting and bring stragglers up to date, you're sending the message that arriving late is okay. And you're also penalizing all the people who cared enough to show up for the meeting on time.

After the meeting

Bureaucrats normally believe that anything anyone says on any topic during a meeting should be recorded. That's fine if the meeting is about legal issues and we need a verbatim transcript. If not, developing highly detailed and comprehensive minutes is normally a waste of time. If Janet attends a two-hour meeting and takes good notes, when the 12-page set of minutes shows up on her desk nine or 10 days later, do you really think she will take the time to read through those minutes? Personally, I don't know *anyone* who reads meeting minutes.

What we need are "One-Minute Minutes." One-Minute Minutes answer the question, "Who is responsible for what, by when?" They also document any decisions reached during the meeting. At the start of the meeting, designate one person to prepare the One-Minute Minutes. The recorder can make copies near the end of the meeting so every person gets a copy on the way out the door.

I once worked in a public sector organization where we held a meeting with 10 mid-level and top-level managers. At the end of the meeting we scheduled a second meeting 30 days later. We also realized that between the first meeting and the second meeting, somebody would have to generate a tremendous amount of information.

At the end of the first meeting, although the discussions had been confusing at times, most of us thought it was clear who had been assigned the responsibility of generating data for the second meeting. But we did not prepare One-Minute

Minutes. So 30 days later, all 10 of us came together from all over the United States. People flew in, rented cars, booked hotel rooms and ate meals, all of which were reimbursable. The next morning the meeting started. The chairperson made some introductory remarks, turned to Mary and said, "Mary, we are ready for your information." Mary's eyes grew to the size of bowling balls. She said, "Me? I thought Frank was responsible." We adjourned. Everybody checked out of the hotel, turned in their cars and flew home. That fiasco cost the American taxpayer in excess of $16,000. What did we accomplish? Absolutely nothing. For lack of what? One-Minute Minutes.

Actions to take now

1. Break away from automatically scheduling an hour for meetings.

2. Start meetings on time and lock the door to encourage punctuality.

3. For every meeting, prepare a Meeting Plan that lists the meeting's purpose, participants (expected contribution), estimated cost, desired outcomes, agenda, date, time and location.

4. Distribute the Meeting Plan three to five days in advance. Use the Meeting Plan during the meeting to keep everyone on track, and write and distribute One-Minute Minutes (a list of who is responsible for what, by when) at the end of each meeting.

9 PROCRASTINATION
How to beat it once and for all

Everyone I know procrastinates — at least once in a while. It's a normal, human tendency. Sometimes procrastination is even smart. We already know that some of the items you initially place on your to-do list will ultimately deserve every bit of procrastination you can give them. They simply won't be important enough to warrant your time and effort. This isn't really procrastination — it's choosing intelligent priorities and recognizing your limits. But how about those times you avoid doing things that truly matter? That's the kind of procrastination that saps your productivity and elevates stress.

For some people it is a relatively minor, though very real problem. For others, procrastination is a devastating personal and professional burden. Fortunately, you can use a number of effective techniques to virtually rid your life of procrastination.

Get the ball rolling

Many people believe that the only victory achieved in combatting procrastination is completing a task. That isn't true. Yes, completing a task is a victory. But so is getting started. When you procrastinate, you're stuck on dead center. You're not moving. So the first victory in your war on procrastination is simply getting the ball rolling. Once it is rolling, then you hope to build up enough momentum to keep the ball rolling until you achieve your second — and final — victory: completing the task. Sometimes, we don't get enough momentum built up and the ball once again comes to a halt. Then we need to regroup and get the ball rolling once more. However, it may take a different technique, or combination of techniques, to get it rolling again. Every time you move forward — no matter how slightly — you need to celebrate your victory. Which brings us to the next point.

Be nice to yourself

When you get going on a task you've been putting off, do something nice for yourself. Take yourself out for dinner. Enjoy a movie. Order dessert, if that's a treat for you. Give yourself a few extra minutes off, or a few extra minutes of relaxation. Reward yourself. When you achieve the ultimate victory by completing the task, reward yourself again. The point is, reward and reinforce yourself for any progress you make. For most of us, procrastination is its own sort of reward — we don't have to do anything. We can be lazy. Turn the tables and make taking action the thing that brings you rewards.

In this chapter, we'll focus on eight different techniques for getting the ball rolling. Each technique is aimed at a slightly different set of circumstances, and you'll need to choose the right technique for each procrastination situation you face.

1. The chunking technique

Have you ever been confronted with a project that was so large and so complex that you couldn't visualize the outcome?

Projects of that magnitude can be completely overwhelming and frustrating. And because you can't visualize the outcome, you have no idea where or how to get started. This is the perfect time to use the chunking technique. This technique will enable you to break down that overwhelming project into smaller, manageable chunks, and will allow you to visualize an outcome. Later, you can concern yourself with integrating the chunks. So, how do you cut down an overwhelming project into smaller chunks? Here are a couple of suggestions:

Chunk by function

Most large projects involve a variety of functions. You may not be able to deal with all the functions simultaneously, but you can probably consider one at a time. Maybe you can tackle the project budget first. Next, maybe you'll want to concentrate on staffing or on production.

Chunk by time

This chunking technique involves dividing the project timeline into smaller increments. Maybe you can't visualize every step in a three-year project, but you probably can see what needs to happen over the next six months. If you combine chunking by time with chunking by function, conquering large projects will become even easier.

Let's consider an example. Suppose your company is planning to open a new production plant and you are responsible for making it happen. You will need to consider long-term requirements in the areas of organizational structure, staffing, budget, logistics support, facilities and so forth. You feel overwhelmed, so you consider the chunking technique. You aren't able to deal with all the functions you've identified today, but could you consider just staffing? Your gut says yes. Great! That's chunking by function. Can you picture staffing requirements for the first five years? Your gut says no. Can you visualize the staffing requirements for the first six months? Sure. The chunking process allows you to get a handle on important parts of the puzzle. Eventually, you'll be able to start putting the whole puzzle together.

2. The time-based attack

The time-based attack is a variation of chunking. Use it when you are facing a large but fairly routine and boring task like filing paperwork. The idea is to select a specific period during which you will furiously file papers. When the time is up, you're allowed to stop and not feel guilty. Stalwart procrastinators love this approach. They can say, "I'm going to file furiously for 10 minutes, then I'm allowed to stop." To carry it a step further and make this technique work best, you must put in your time today, then tomorrow you must do it again — and the day after that too. By the fourth day, you might find yourself filing without any time limit. Why? Because the stack is shrinking pretty fast, you're making headway, you're building momentum, and the task really wasn't as bad as you had imagined.

3. The spark plug technique

Have you ever had to write a response to a complaining customer? Did you find yourself a little reluctant to write that letter, particularly if your company was in the wrong? Writing this type of letter is easy to put off because it is unpleasant and embarrassing. The spark plug technique is an easy way to get yourself moving. In order to write the response letter, you probably have to pull the customer's file and review it. The spark plug technique involves the process of pulling the file and putting it on your desk in front of you. Merely pulling a file isn't unpleasant or embarrassing. Now, of course, the file is in your way. So you read the complaint again, and soon you find yourself jotting down a few notes about how to respond. Next thing you know, you have drafted and edited your response and it's in the mail. What got things moving? The spark of doing a mindless, physical act just to get the ball rolling.

4. Using a balance sheet

To create a procrastination balance sheet, take a piece of paper and draw a line down the middle of the page. Label the top left "Reasons for Procrastinating" and label the top right "Reasons for Getting Started." With all these reasons in your mind, which list do you think is usually longest and strongest? Clearly the left one — and that's why you have successfully procrastinated so far. Those reasons for procrastinating sound awfully good — as long as they stay in your head. But when you actually write your reasons for procrastinating on the balance sheet, they start looking pretty pathetic. In fact, the left column turns out to be short and weak and the right column becomes long and strong. Seeing the tremendous imbalance in favor of getting started is usually enough to get most procrastinators moving.

5. The wheat-from-the-chaff technique

Use the wheat-from-the-chaff-technique primarily for philosophically important matters in your life, those that have relatively high emotional consequences. Often, when you are highly involved in one of these important matters, you find yourself too close to the forest to see the trees. Examples: Should I keep this job or quit? Should I stay in this career or not? Should I make this heavy financial investment? Should I get married? Should we separate or get divorced? Should we have another child?

When you find yourself too close to those kinds of issues, you lose clarity. You can't recognize and analyze all the facts, all the pros and cons. When you're faced with an important issue or life decision, take an old tablet or notebook and write down whatever thoughts and emotions you have about the issue. Don't worry about being logical. Don't worry about how few or how many thoughts or emotions you write down. Don't worry about their initial priority. Just get them all down on paper.

Once you've recorded every thought you can imagine about the topic and every feeling you've experienced — good or bad, strong or weak — then, and only then, assign priority codes to each item. Prioritizing your thoughts and emotions will quickly help you sort out the most crucial issues. The clouds will clear. With clarity, decision making is much easier.

6. The broadcast technique

When it comes to changing major habits — quitting smoking, going on a diet, starting a long-term exercise program, etc. — the broadcast technique is extremely valuable. The premise is simple: Tell everybody what you're doing. After I quit smoking, I mentioned my accomplishment in every seminar that I presented the next six months. I mentioned it intentionally because I needed a lot of motivation to keep myself from going back to smoking. You see, I knew that someday I would be back at one of the places where I had made a presentation and somebody, somewhere would come up to me and say, "Last time you were here, Dick, you said you quit smoking. Did you make it stick?" And I knew that one day I would have tremendous satisfaction in being able to say, "Yeah, it stuck."

Sure enough, in Alexandria, VA, six months after I quit, a woman who had been in one of my seminars six months earlier came up to me and said, "You said you quit; did you completely quit?" And I was able to say, "Yes." I learned that broadcasting and putting a little pressure on yourself makes good sense and can be a powerful motivator.

7. Worst first

Have you ever had one of those difficult, complex and boring, but very important projects sitting on your desk? You're supposed to be working on it. And every single day you promise yourself that you're going to work on it. But you don't. You make promises to yourself: I'm going to work on it right before I go home today. Of course, at the end of the day you're exhausted, your attitude's shot, your energy's gone, and you're not going to work on that difficult, boring, complex task. So you promise yourself that the next day, right before you go home, you will work on it. And you don't. The process goes on and on.

The worst-first technique is unquestionably the best way to break the cycle of procrastination. Simply do the worst thing — the most difficult task, the hardest project to face — first. Use a block of prime time early in the morning (if you're an early morning starter) to conquer those worst-first projects. Nail the toughest projects early in the morning because if you knock them out early in the day, you'll have a better attitude for the rest of the day, and all your other tasks will be easier to handle. Mark Twain understood the worst-first concept. He suggested, "If you're going to have to swallow a live frog, don't look at it too long."

8. Affirmations

Because procrastination is such a destructive force, most people need lots of positive input to overcome it. Affirmations will offset the negativism generated by procrastination. Keep positive reminders in front of you — on your desk, your computer monitor, your bathroom mirror, your refrigerator, and in your briefcase. These positive reminders, or affirmations, will give you the incentive you need to move forward. Here are some examples:

- The door to success is labeled "push."

- Success comes in rising every time you fall.

- There is no failure except in no longer trying.

- There is never so tragic a loss as a talent left dormant or one grown stale from lack of effort.

- The man who says it can't be done is liable to be knocked down by someone doing it.

- Leaders are like turtles — they can go forward only when their necks are out.

Procrastination can ruin your life

Procrastination is like a disease. It gets worse with time if we don't do something positive about it. I had two very close friends who let procrastination ruin their lives. One lost his family as a result of procrastination. The other lost his career. Procrastination will affect everyone around you. If you try to use the techniques in this chapter, and find that after three to six months none of them have worked for you, you may have a much deeper problem and should seriously consider seeking professional help. Be brutally honest with yourself in analyzing how much procrastination is holding you back.

Action steps to take now

1. Get the ball rolling, then reward yourself.

2. Break down large projects into small tasks.

3. Use the mindless lead-in task in the spark plug technique, and draw upon the procrastination balance sheet to get you started.

4. For very important matters in your life, separate the wheat from the chaff. Keep a journal and prioritize your thoughts and emotions to aid in decision making.

5. When you decide to change major habits, use the broadcast technique to enlist support for your efforts.

6. For those difficult, complex and boring projects, use the worst-first technique.

7. Surround yourself with affirmations to help overcome procrastination's negative force.

10 CONCLUSION
The time of your life

You are more valuable than all the time in the world

If you've gained anything at all from this book, I hope it is this: Time management has two distinct faces. One is its practical side — the tools, techniques, worksheets and exercises. The other side of effective time management is philosophical — your beliefs about the value and limits of time, and your own willingness to change these beliefs. There's no way around it — even with all the timesaving techniques in this book, no one will ever succeed in inventing a 25-hour day. Taking control of your time and your life means taking control of *what matters*. And if you've read this book with care, you know that not everything does matter.

Without question, however, *you* matter. You are a valuable individual, above and beyond the sum of all the tasks you complete in a day. Think of time management as something that makes *you* feel good, not only as a way to get more done. Does that sound a little selfish? Well, it's not.

Because when you're strangled by conflicting priorities and endless demands on your time, you're not much use to others around you. Frankly, poor time managers are often less available to others than efficient time managers are, because they're always absorbed in a crisis. Managing your time wisely is one of the best ways I know to remind yourself that you matter. Do it to regain balance in your life — to reclaim peace of mind. Do it because you enjoy the control and confidence it brings you — not merely to churn out more work every day. Manage your time wisely because *you matter.* I wish you success.

BIBLIOGRAPHY

Books

Breaking Your Time Barrier: Becoming a Strategic Time Manager. Ross A. Webber. Old Tappan, NJ: Prentice Hall, 1991.

Breathing Space: Living and Working at a Comfortable Pace in a Sped-Up Society. Jeff Davidson. New York: Master Media Ltd., 1991.

Commonsense Time Management. New York: AMACOM, 1992.

Delegating for Results. Robert B. Maddux. Menlo Park, CA: Crisp Publications, 1990.

Doing It Now. Edwin C. Bliss. New York: Charles Scribner's Sons, 1983.

First Things First. Stephen R. Covey, Roger A. Merrill and Rebecca R. Merrill. New York: Simon & Schuster, 1994.

How You Can Move Beyond Procrastination. Virginia M. Granger. Tempe, AZ: Moving On Publications, 1991.

Procrastination: Why You Do It. What to Do About It. Jane B. Burka. Reading, MA: Addison-Wesley, 1990.

Right on Time: The Complete Guide for Time-Pressured Managers.
Lester R. Bittel. New York: McGraw, 1990.

Seize the Day! How to Best Use What Can't Be Replaced — Time.
Michael F. Woolery. Oklahoma City, OK: Time Link, 1991.

*SoftPower! How to Speak Up, Set Limits & Say No Without Losing
Your Job, Your Lover or Your Friends.* Maria Arapakis.
New York: Warner Books, 1990.

Tapes

Controlling Interruptions (video). Verne Harnish.
Boulder, CO: CareerTrack Publications, 1987/1989.

How to Delegate Work and Ensure It's Done Right (audio/video).
Dick Lohr. Boulder, CO: CareerTrack Publications, 1992.

How to Speak Up, Set Limits and Say No (audio). Maria Arapakis.
Boulder, CO: CareerTrack Publications, 1986.

How to Interview and Hire the Right People (video). Stephen Carline.
Boulder, CO: CareerTrack Publications, 1992.

Stress Skills for Turbulent Times (audio). Roger Mellott.
Boulder, CO: CareerTrack Publications, 1995.

Succeeding as a First-Time Manager (audio /video). Dick Lohr.
Boulder, CO: CareerTrack Publications, 1995.

Success Shortcuts (audio). James Calano and Jeff Salzman.
Boulder, CO: CareerTrack Publications, 1985.

Taking Control of Your Workday (audio/video). Dick Lohr.
Boulder, CO: CareerTrack Publications, 1992.